JN102660

Attention All Sports Fans !

Mark Thompson

Toshihiro Tanioka

EIHŌSHA

テキストの音声は、弊社 HP
http://www.eihosha.co.jp/の
「テキスト音声ダウンロード」
のバナーからダウンロードでき
ます。

はじめに

　本書は、平易な英語で身近な話題であるスポーツとアスリートについて学ぶと共に、英文法の基礎の学び直しを主眼にしたテキストです。

身近な話題のスポーツ

　スポーツは世界中の多くの人達にとって最も身近な話題の一つです。時代、国境は勿論、人種・民族、宗教・宗派等の差異を越えて多くの老若男女に親しまれています。また、スポーツは、その観衆、ファン等に感動、元気、勇気、希望、夢等を与えます。そしてスポーツは、メディアを始め家庭、職場、学校、通勤や通学時、社交の場、旅先等でも話題になります。日本においては 2019 年秋、アジアで初めて開催されたラグビーワールドカップ時の熱狂ぶりはまだ記憶に新しく、新しいヒーローが誕生しラグビーの理解者やファンを増やしました。

　そうしたスポーツとアスリートについて、平易な英語で親しみ、学び、英語学習の一助にして欲しいという思いから本書を著しました。スポーツといっても多々あり、またスターアスリートも多くいます。紙幅の制約上、本書ではアメリカのプロ野球 MLB（通称メジャーリーグ）、アメリカのプロバスケットボール（NBA）等のスポーツと複数の新星とベテランのアスリートを扱うにとどめました。これだけでもバラエティに富み、学生には今まで以上に英語の授業に前向きになってもらえるのでは、と期待しています。

英文法との仲直り

　スポーツをはじめ、何事においても、その基礎が大事であることは論を待ちません。最近、リメディアル教育という言葉を時々、耳にします。一部の高等教育機関において、既習科目の基礎の再教育の必要性が高まってきているように感じます。入試制度や高等教育の大衆化等がその背景にあると思われます。実際、公開されているシラバスからも窺えるように、リメディアル教育に取り組んでいる高等教育機関も少なくないのです。英語教育も例外ではありません。

　そこで、このテキストには英文法の基礎の学び直し "**Back to Basics**" というもう一つの柱を持たせました。英語の基礎文法の再確認です。英文法と聞くと、「苦手」「もう十分」「退屈」「嫌い」等と否定的な受け止め方をする人も少なくないでしょう。「（英語は）話せればいい。文法はいらない。」という意見も時々、耳にします。しかし、会話でも、相手の考えや発言を正確に理解し、自分の考えを正確に伝えるには、やはり英文法の基礎は不可欠です。また、日本人は何年も英語を学んでいるにもかかわらず、簡単な英会話もできないとよく言われます。英語の基礎、英文法の基礎の未習得がその一因とも考えられます。英語の基本文法と仲直りをし、その学び直しをしましょう。

これらを踏まえ、このテキストには以下のような特徴を持たせています。

・半期完結用の全 15 ユニットの構成。毎回扱うトピックを独立させ、学生は、毎授業、新鮮な気持ちで授業に取り組めます。

・各ユニットは、バランスの取れた構成で、1 ユニットは 1 演習（90 分）で完結。一応、本文理解に 40 分、聴解に 10 分、英語の基礎の解説・確認に 20 分、Exercise に 20 分を目安としています。しかし、本文の予習を課し、聴解は割愛する等、その時間配分には、工夫の余地があると思います。

・本文理解には、その指針となる複数の具体的な質問（Q）と豊富な語（句）等のヒント。辞書で単語を引く手間が省け本文の内容把握がよりスムーズにできるように配慮しました。

・聴解練習は、問題文以外はテキストに記載した選択肢からの解答形式。英検のリスニング問題形式を模しました。

・ポイントを絞った基礎文法のまとめ。その理解の確認は、簡単な練習問題で行います。英作問題は語順を問う基礎問題と、やや難度を上げて語彙力、文法力、表現・作文力を問う自由英作の 2 部構成で英作の苦手な学生と基礎問題で物足りない学生の両方に対応。そのユニットの基礎文法の習熟度を高める工夫をしました。

・ハーフ・タイムや Coffee Break。スポーツ関連の英語の豆知識、扱ったスポーツやアスリートに関するエピソードは学生の授業への好奇心を喚起し、その維持と向上に期待が持てます。

・豊富なイラストと写真。視覚面からも理解度と興味を高める工夫をしました。

　こうした特長を持たせた本書が、身近なスポーツという話題を通して、学生の英語への関心と英語の基礎力アップの一助になれば幸いです。

　最後に、本書の出版に賛同して下さった英宝社社長の佐々木　元氏と、編集、校正段階で大変お世話になった同社編集部の下村　幸一氏に心から謝意を表します。
　新型コロナウイルス禍の影響で本書の執筆も思うように進まない時期がありました。しかし、同社のご高配のお陰でなんとか今年、本書も上梓に漕ぎつけることができました。

2020 年 晩秋　　　　　　　著　者

Contents

Attention All Sports Fans !

Unit 1　Major League Baseball

I　Vocabulary Checking

A群の英単語の日本語訳をB群より選びその記号を［　　］に記入しなさい。

◆A群

1 charge 　　［　　］　　2 current 　　［　　］　　3 retire 　　　［　　］

4 pastime 　　［　　］　　5 legendary ［　　］

◆B群

a 娯楽　　**b** 伝説の　　**c** 現在の　　**d**（料金を）請求する　　**e** 引退する

II　Reading

☆ **Before Reading Passage**(Q［質問・指針］を念頭に passage［本文］を読んでみましょう)

Q1 野球の起源とアメリカでの普及について読み取りましょう。また、ベーブ・ルースとは誰のことですか？

Q2「野球殿堂（博物館）」について読み取りましょう。（いつ創設、何処、展示内容、イチローとの関係等）

Q3 今日の MLB（アメリカのプロ野球）の概略─リーグ数、チーム数、ワールドシリーズとは等。

☆ **Words & Phrases**（単語、語句のヒント）

1 originate 始まる　　2 soldiers 兵士　　3 spectators 観客　　4 plaques 額　　5 inspire ～を勇気づける

☆ **Passage**

　The U.S. does not have a national sport, but baseball is America's national **pastime**. Who invented this popular sport? Its origin is not quite clear. Some believe that Abner Doubleday invented it in Cooperstown, New York back in 1839. Some others say that it [1]originated in Great Britain much earlier than this.

　There is no doubt that baseball has been quite a popular sport in America. In the early 1860s, some [2]soldiers enjoyed baseball as recreation during the[注1]Civil War. After the war, they helped to spread the sport nationwide after returning to their hometowns. Some teams in this era started **charging** [3]spectators, which marked the beginning of professional baseball. Major League Baseball (MLB), the **current** professional baseball organization formed in 1903, is the oldest professional sports organization in the United States.

　Like other professional sports, baseball has produced some **legendary** star players. Babe Ruth, the "Home Run King", set the lifetime home run record of[注2]714 in 1935. Ruth also played as a pitcher. It is fresh on our minds that in 2004 Japanese player Ichiro Suzuki of the Seatle Mariners set the MLB single season hitting record of 262 hits.

In 1939, the National Baseball Hall of Fame and Museum was created in Cooperstown. They display the famous star players' [4]plaques, uniforms, gloves and bats, including Ichiro's bat. Many baseball fans were greatly shocked to learn Ichiro's announcement to **retire** from his baseball career in 2019 in Japan. No doubt Ichiro's great career in MLB has [5]inspired other baseball players inside and outside MLB and will continue to do so.

Currently, MLB has two leagues the American League and the National League. There are thirty teams; 29 in America and one in Canada. Each team plays more than 160 games a year and at the end of the season, they hold the World Series, the annual championship series. As of 2020 the New York Yankees have won the most titles, 27.

注1　the Civil War －南北戦争（1861-1865 年）。主に黒人奴隷制の是非を争点に南部（奴隷制の維持に賛成）と北部（奴隷制反対）に２分裂し戦った戦争。北部が勝利し、黒人はリンカーン大統領の奴隷解放宣言（1863 年１月）で奴隷から解放された。

注2　現在は 2007 年、バリー ボンズが樹立した 762 本が MLB の記録。

Ⅲ Listening Comprehension

Listen to the CD and choose the correct answer about the passage.

1　A　in Great Britain

　　B　It is not clear.

　　C　Mr. Doubleday did.

2　A　Ichiro's teammate in the Seatle Mariners

　　B　He was once a home run king.

　　C　He is the New York Yankees' manager who retired in 1935.

3　A　Abner Doubleday was born in the city and invented baseball.

　　B　At the end of the season, they hold the World Series there.

　　C　The Baseball Hall of Fame was built there in 1939.

4　A　Each MLB team plays 160 games a year.

　　B　Not all MLB teams are in the U.S.

　　C　Ichiro's bat is in the Baseball Hall of Fame and Museum.

Answers　1＿＿＿＿＿＿　2＿＿＿＿＿＿　3＿＿＿＿＿＿　4＿＿＿＿＿＿

ハーフタイム

☆野球英語表現の豆知識 ♪♪

| 日　本　語 | 表 / 裏 | ゴロ | ファウル |
| 英　　　語 | top / bottom | grounder | *foul |

　　　　＊ a foul play ☞ 野球やソフトボールのファウルと同じ語だが foul play は
　　　　①反則　②犯罪（特に殺人）という意味でも使われる。

Ⅳ　Back to Basics（英文法の基礎）①　be 動詞

・ポイント 1 ☞ be 動詞には be（原形）、is、am, are（以上現在形）、was、were（過去形）
　　　　と been（過去分詞）がある。主な意味 ➜ 現在形：〜です、〜である。
　　　　過去形：〜であった、〜でした等。

主　　　語	be 動詞(現在)	be 動詞(過去)	例　　　　　　　　文
I	am	was	I am / was a rich man.
You	are	were	You are / were a famous baseball player.
He, Tom, She, Sue 等	is	was	Tom / She is / was an English teacher.
It, 単数の動物、物等	is	was	It is a new cell phone / My cat is cute.
We, You（君達）, They Tom and Mary 等複数	are	were	We / You / They are / were happy.

・ポイント 2 ☞ be 動詞が原形（be）で使われるケース ☞ 助動詞の後、命令文等。
　　　　例文　It will be rainy tomorrow.（明日は、雨になるでしょう）。/ Be quiet.
　　　　（静かにしなさい）。

・ポイント 3 ☞ 疑問文は、be 動詞を主語の前に置く。否定文は、その be 動詞の後ろに
　　　　not をつける。
　　　　例文　疑問文 Are you a student?　否定文 He is not（又は isn't）rich.
　　　　　　　　　　　　　　　　　　　　　You are not（aren't）sick.
　　　　　　　Is he rich?　　　　　　　　　He was not（wasn't）at the
　　　　　　　　　　　　　　　　　　　　　party yesterday.
　　　　　　　Were you tired then?　　　　We were not（weren't）at home
　　　　　　　　　　　　　　　　　　　　　then.

4

Exercise 1　次の各英文の（　＊　）に入る適当な be 動詞を下の解答欄に記入しなさい。

1　My sister（　＊　）a college student.

2　I（　＊　）happy to meet you.

3　There（　＊　）only two hotels in this city ten years ago.

4　I am happy that you and I（　＊　）in the same class this year.

5　（　＊　）you at home last Sunday?

6　We are hungry.（　＊　）dinner ready?

7　Mary,（　＊　）you from New York?

8　Two plus three（　＊　）five.

Answers

1＿＿＿＿　2＿＿＿＿　3＿＿＿＿　4＿＿＿＿　5＿＿＿＿　6＿＿＿＿　7＿＿＿＿　8＿＿＿＿

Exercise 2　1と2は［　　　］内の語（句）を並べ替え、3～5は日本文にあう英文を各々書いてみましょう。　　　（注：文頭の文字と句読点は、要適宜対応）

1　ここからそのホテルまでの距離はどれくらい？

[is, to, far, the hotel, here, it, how, from]?

➜＿＿＿＿＿＿＿＿＿＿＿＿＿＿＿＿＿＿＿＿＿＿＿＿＿＿＿＿＿＿＿＿＿＿＿

2　今朝は曇りだったが今は晴れている。

[was, fine, it, cloudy, now, but, it, this morning, is]

➜＿＿＿＿＿＿＿＿＿＿＿＿＿＿＿＿＿＿＿＿＿＿＿＿＿＿＿＿＿＿＿＿＿＿＿

3　私の叔父は弁護士で、私は高校教員です。

➜＿＿＿＿＿＿＿＿＿＿＿＿＿＿＿＿＿＿＿＿＿＿＿＿＿＿＿＿＿＿＿＿＿＿＿

4　私の両親は大学教授です。母はアメリカ人でハワイ生まれです。

➜＿＿＿＿＿＿＿＿＿＿＿＿＿＿＿＿＿＿＿＿＿＿＿＿＿＿＿＿＿＿＿＿＿＿＿

5　「先々週、君が一週間の休暇で京都にいた時、お天気はどうだった？」
　　「運悪く良くなかったね。ほぼ毎日雨だったよ。」

➜＿＿＿＿＿＿＿＿＿＿＿＿＿＿＿＿＿＿＿＿＿＿＿＿＿＿＿＿＿＿＿＿＿＿＿

Coffee Break I

ヤンキー・スタジアムは、ベーブ・ルースが建てた？

　メジャー・リーグ名門チームのニューヨーク・ヤンキーズの本拠地である（旧）ヤンキー・スタジアムは、ニューヨーク市のブロンクス地区にあった。日本のプロ野球選手の松井秀喜やイチローらが所属していたことで日本でも話題になり、野球ファンでなくとも聞いたことはあるのではないだろうか。

　同球場ができたのは 1923 年。近くの既存の野球場でヤンキーズが人気を博し連日大入りだったことで新球場の必要性が高まり、ヤンキーズのための野球場を建設することになったという。これほどまでにファンを魅了したのが、1920 年にボストンのレッド・ソックスから移籍した MLB 伝説の人、アメリカン・ヒーロー、野球の神様の異名をとるベーブ・ルースだった。 The house that Babe Ruth built.（ベーブ・ルースが建てた球場）と言われる所以である。（出典 Brad Herzog。The Sports 100. p.20. Macmillan 他）

　この年、ベーブ・ルースはヤンキー・スタジアム最初のホームランを放ち、シーズンを 41 本のホームランと 3 割 9 分 3 厘の高打率で終えた。ファンを魅了し、期待に応える形でシーズンを終えた。

　なお、現ヤンキー・スタジアムは、2009 年に完成したもの。

Unit 2　Shohei Ohtani - It's Sho Time!

photo by Erik Drost

I　Vocabulary Checking

A群の英単語の日本語訳をB群より選びその記号を［　　］に記入しなさい。

◆A群

1 consideration ［　　］　　2 notable ［　　］　　3 amazing ［　　］

4 consistently ［　　］　　5 contract ［　　］

◆B群

a 目立つ　　**b** 素晴らしい　　**c** ずっと、不変で　　**d** 熟慮　　**e** 契約（する）

II　Reading

☆ **Before Reading Passage**（Q［質問・指針］を念頭に passage［本文］を読んでみましょう）

Q1 大谷翔平選手の野球選手としての最大の特徴は何でしょうか。

Q2 大谷選手の日本ハムファイターズ時代の活躍ぶり、また記録について読み取りましょう。

Q3 大谷選手の MLB（アメリカのプロ野球）での 2020 年までの活躍ぶりをふり返ってみましょう。

☆ **Words & Phrases**（単語、語句のヒント）

1 phenomenal 脅威的な　2 standout 傑出した　3 rack up 築く　4 rewarding 価値ある　5 appearances 登板

☆ **Passage**

Shohei Ohtani is a truly remarkable professional baseball player. His career so far has been nothing short of [1]phenomenal.

Ohtani was born in 1994 and raised in Oshu in Iwate Prefecture. He attended Hanamaki Higashi High School. His talent as a [2]standout defensive and offensive player became obvious during these early years in school. He was able to pitch a baseball 160 km/h. That was **amazing** for a high schooler.

There was a lot of interest from MLB teams to sign him directly out of high school. He thought he might turn pro in the U.S. After some **consideration**, however, in December 2012 Ohtani signed a **contract** to play for the Hokkaido Nippon-Ham Fighters. He started as an outfielder and a pitcher. Due to his great popularity among fans in his rookie year, he was voted to play on the Pacific League All-Star team. In fact, he was voted to the All-Star Team every year in his five years of playing professional baseball in Japan, [3]racking up a number of **notable** records. For example, he recorded the fastest pitch ever thrown in[注1]NPB with a ball speed of 165 km/h. In 2015, he led the Pacific League in wins and winning percentage with a 15–5 record in just 22 starts. He also received the Pacific League MVP award in 2016. After five productive and [4]rewarding seasons playing with the Fighters, Ohtani signed in December 2017 a contract to play for the Los Angeles Angels in the Major Leagues.

In his rookie year of the 2018 season, Ohtani impressed a lot of U.S. baseball fans as a two-way player, pitcher and outfielder. He hit 22 homeruns and 4 wins as a pitcher. He joined Babe Ruth as the only two MLB players with 10 pitching [5]appearances and over 20 homeruns in a season. Ohtani won the American League Rookie of the Month award two times, first in April and then in September. At the end of his first season in MLB, Ohtani was named the American League Rookie of the Year! Although surgery on his right elbow in October 2018 put his role as a pitcher on hold the next season, Ohtani kept impressing his fans by[注2]hitting for the cycle and 18 homeruns as a designated hitter. Recovering from the surgery, Ohtani returned as a two-way player in the 2020 season. In 2020, MLB added two-way players as the sixth position to the existing five positions.

Having realized his dream to play in MLB, Shohei's future as a star player looks quite bright. His legacy depends on his ability to **consistently** play well and to avoid a career-ending injury.

注1 NPB Nippon Professional Baseball 日本（プロ）野球機構
注2 hit for the cycle 1試合で本塁打、三塁打、二塁打、シングルヒットの４本を打つこと。

III Listening Comprehension

Listen to the CD and choose the correct answer about the passage.

1 A more than twenty
  B Yes, Babe Ruth is quite famous as a homerun batter in America.
  C He hit 18 homeruns as a designated hitter in 2019.

2 A He decided to play professional in Japan in 2012.
  B He played for the Hokkaido Nippon-Ham Fighters for five years.
  C Yes, some MLB. teams as well as Japanese teams wanted to sign him.

3 A The Los Angeles Angels did.
  B Yes, Ohtani first wanted to turn professional in America.
  C It is not clear from the passage.

4 A The Los Angeles Angels have had 2 two-way players, Ohtani and Babe Ruth.
  B Shohei did not play as a pitcher in his second year for the Los Angeles Angels.
  C Ohtani's rookie years in Japan and in America were both remarkable.

Answers 1 _____ 2 _____ 3 _____ 4 _____

ハーフタイム

☆ **major** は メジャ じゃ 駄目ジャ？ ☺

　アメリカのプロ野球 MLB（Major League Baseball）の major は「専攻（する)」「主な」「多数の」等の意味がある語。

　ところで、その発音は、敢えてカタカナ書きすると、メジャ（ー）ではなくメイジャ（ー）。

メジャ（ー）と発音すると別単語の measure「物差し、はかり」「〜を測る」に聞こえるようだ。英語で使用し発音するときは誤解されないように注意したい。

Ⅳ　Back to Basics（英文法の基礎）②　動詞・時制1（現在形）

・ポイント **1**　動作を表わす語を動詞と言う。原形、過去形、過去分詞と変化する。

	規則変化をする動詞の例				不規則変化をする /変化をしない動詞の例				
原　　形	play	study	plan	live	run	speak	sing	have/has	cut
過 去 形	played	studied	planned	lived	ran	spoke	sang	had	cut
過去分詞	played	studied	planned	lived	run	spoken	sung	had	cut

・ポイント **2**　現在時制の動詞の基本である "三単現の s（又は es）" とは？

　　主語が、三人称、かつ単数で、その文の時制が現在の場合、その文の動詞の語尾に "**s**" 又は "**es**" がつくルール。

　　☞ 一人称は I と we、二人称は you、三人称は一人称、二人称以外全てで he, she, they, it, Tom、my car 等

　　例文　Tom plays soccer every day. / It snows here every winter. / Our cat loves milk.
　　　　　（Tom ☞ 三人称で単数）　　　　　　（It ☞ 同左）　　　　　（Our cat ☞ 同左）

・ポイント **3**　疑問文は **do（does）** を主語の前に置き、否定文は **do not（don't）/ does（doesn't）** 等を動詞の前に置く。

　　・肯定文 You play soccer on Sundays.　　　Tom plays soccer after school.
　　・疑問文 Do you play soccer on Sundays?　　Does Tom play soccer after school?
　　・否定文 You do not（don't）play soccer on Sundays. Tom does not（doesn't）play soccer after school.

Exercise 1　次の各英文の（　　）内の語を必要があれば、適当な語に変え下の解答欄に記入しなさい。

　1 My older brother（speak）English very well.
　2（Do）your grandpa have a smart phone?
　3 Mr. Smith（teach）us English.
　4 I sometimes（help）our father wash his car.
　5 My father（don' t）drive but he enjoys biking.
　6 The city（have）three parks.

Answers

1＿＿＿＿＿　2＿＿＿＿＿　3＿＿＿＿＿　4＿＿＿＿＿　5＿＿＿＿＿　6＿＿＿＿＿

Exercise 2　1と2は［　　］内の語（句）を並べ替え、3～5は日本文にあう英文を
各々書いてみましょう。　　　（注：文頭の文字と句読点は、要適宜対応）

1　私の母は花が大好きで庭で多くのバラの花を育てています。

　　［grows, and, the garden, flowers, my mother, roses, loves, in, a lot of］

→_____

2　その試験に落ちたくなければ、もっと一生懸命勉強する必要があるよ。

　　You［want, harder, don't, to, the exam, if, need to , you, study, fail］

→_____

3　予約はしていませんが、今夜私が泊まる部屋ありますか。

→_____

4　父は煙草は吸いませんが、時々お酒やビールは飲みます。

→_____

5　もし提案をお受になるなら同封の用紙を今月末までに返送ください。

　　　　　　　　　　　　　　　　　　　　　　［ヒント：用紙 ☞ form］

→_____

Coffee Break 2

チーム名と都市の関係

　アメリカのプロスポーツのチーム名には、そのチームの本拠地の都市の特徴と関係がある名前がある。

　アメリカ中西部にあるウィスコンシン州ミルウォーキー市の MLB チームのミルウォーキーブルワーズは同市の醸造産業を反映したものである（ブルワーズ＝brewers とはビール等を醸造する人、会社の意味）。同都市には全米でも有数のビール醸造会社であるミラー・ブルイング会社の本社がある。19 世紀にビール好きの多くのドイツ系移民が移住して定住したこのウィスコンシン州でビール産業が発展したのも自然なことであった。現在、同州の人口の 40％以上をドイツ系が占める。

　別の MLB チームのヒューストン・アストロズも、本拠地テキサス州ヒューストン市にあり、似た例である。最初、同チームはヒューストン・コルトと呼ばれていた。しかし、このヒューストンに NASA（米国航空宇宙局）の宇宙センターが置かれると、同都市の宇宙開発計画への支援の意味を込めてアストロズ（astronauts［宇宙飛行士］の短縮）と 1965 年 4 月に改名されたのである。

　本拠地に住む地元ファンは居住する都市の特徴や歴史を思い起こしながら地元チームの応援をするのである。

Unit 3 The NBA

I   Vocabulary Checking

A群の英単語の日本語訳を B 群より選びその記号を［　　］に記入しなさい。

◆ A群

1 deivise ［　　］　　　2 locals ［　　］　　　3 merge ［　　］

4 elevate ［　　］　　　5 intercollegiate ［　　］

◆ B群

a 地域住民　　**b** 大学間の　　**c** ～を考案する　　**d** 合併する　　**e** ～を引き上げる

II   Reading

CD
6

☆ **Before Reading Passage**(Q［質問・指針］を念頭に passage［本文］を読んでみましょう)

Q1 バスケットボールの始まりは？(いつ、どこで、何のために、誰によって考案され、また変化、発展したか等)

Q2 バスケットボールは米国の大学にどのように普及したか？また、対抗試合の開催について読み取りましょう。

Q3 NBA の始まりや変化、伝説の NBA 選手、現在の規模(リーグ、チーム数、試合数等)について読み取りましょう。

☆ **Words & Phrases** （単語、語句のヒント）

1 physical education 体育　　　2 initially 最初は　　　3 standout 傑出した　　　4 legendary 伝説の

☆ **Passage**

Basketball is a sport of American invention. It was **devised** in the winter of 1891-92 by Dr. James Naismith, a [1]physical education teacher at YMCA Training College in Springfield, [注1]Massachusetts. Dr. Naismith invented it as an inter-season sport that could be played indoors in winter. [2]Initially, teams had nine players each, but five became standard several years later. Basketball required much less space than baseball or football, which helped it to become popular in cities. Basketball quickly spread across the nation and became the most widely attended indoor spectator sport in America.

College basketball became more and more popular after the turn of the century. In 1939, they started the **intercollegiate** national tournament. Today, major American colleges have their own indoor sport arenas on campus, many of which can accommodate more than 10,000 fans. Intercollegiate basketball games are usually held on campus and many students and **locals** as well as players can enjoy or play games in the middle of winter regardless of the weather. [3]Standout college players move up to play at the professional level in the[注2]National Basketball Association (NBA).

The NBA officially started in 1949 with seventeen teams after two existing professional leagues **merged**. In NBA history, the 1980s is called the golden era. The three-point field goal introduced in 1979 helped raise popularity of basketball. Also in that year, two [4]legendary players, Earvin Magic Johnson from Michigan State University and Larry Bird from Indiana State University joined the Los Angeles Lakers and the Boston Celtics respectively. As expected, their rivalry in the 1980s excited many basketball fans. Joining them later in this decade was another legendary star player Michael Jordan who played for the Chicago Bulls. These players known as the superstar players of all time helped to **elevate** popularity of professional basketball more than ever before.

As of 2020, there are thirty NBA teams, twenty-nine in the U.S. and one in Toronto, Canada. The regular season lasts from October to April with each team playing eighty-two games a year. The Boston Celtics have won the most NBA championships with 17 titles.

注 1 Massachusetts マサチューセッツ州 米国北東部の州。州都はボストンで郊外にはハーバード大学がある。

注 2 National Basketball Associaion（NBA）米国プロバスケットボール協会（前身の Basketball Association of America［BAA］は 1946 年設立）

III Listening Comprehension

CD
7

Listen to the CD and choose the correct answer about the passage.

1 A He was an English teacher at YMCA College.

   B He was a teacher at YMCA Training College.

   C Yes, he invented basketball as an indoor sport.

2 A Yes, it became popular after the turn of the century.

   B Because it required less space than baseball and football.

   C It was invented in the winter of 1891-1892.

3 A They can play games in the middle of winter regardless of weather.

   B College superstar players continue to play in the NBA.

   C their own indoor sport arenas

4 A There are 30 teams in the NBA and they are all in the United States.

   B The three-point field goal introduced in 1979 was helpful to make basketball more popular.

   C Earvin Magic Johnson and Larry Bird were good rivals in the 1980s.

Answers 1 _____ 2 _____ 3 _____ 4 _____

ハーフタイム

☆ **Larry Bird** と **Earvin Magic Johnson**

　本文でも登場したこの二人は、学生時代からのライバルだった。1979 年、ほぼ同時に別々の NBA チーム（本文参照）と契約した。それぞれ、MVP を 3 回（Bird は 1984-1986 年、Johnson は 1987, 1989-1990 年）受賞した。

IV　Back to Basics（英文法の基礎）③　動詞・時制2（過去形＆未来形）

- ・ポイント 1　過去形 ☞ 規則動詞は動詞の後に "ed" をつける。不規則動詞は、それぞれ変化する。
  例 play-played, study-studied, live-lived / sing-sang, speak-spoke, have-had
- ・ポイント 2　未来形 ☞ 原形動詞の前に will を置く。will の代りに be going to で代用可能な場合あり。
- ・ポイント 3　疑問文 ☞ 過去形（時制）は did で、未来形（時制）は will で表す。
- ・ポイント 4　否定文 ☞ 過去形は did not（didn't）で、未来形は will not（won't）で表す。

	過去時制の例文	未来時制の例文
・肯定文	You played golf yesterday.	Tom will play baseball this afternoon.
・疑問文	Did you play golf yesterday?	Will Tom play baseball this afternoon?
・否定文	You did not（didn't）play golf yesterday.	Tom will not（won't）play baseball this afternoon.

Exercise 1 次の各英文の（　　）内から適当な語（句）を選び、その記号を下の解答
欄に記入しなさい。

1 Did you (ア study　イ studied　ウ were study　エ do study) English last night?
2 We (ア heard　イ hear　ウ were heard　エ did heard) a strange sound in front of the door then.
3 She (ア will busy　イ will be busy　ウ will is busy　エ is going to busy) tomorrow.
4 (ア Do　イ Does　ウ Did　エ Was) Mary cut her finger while she was cooking last night?
5 My uncle (ア coming　イ will coming　ウ will be come　エ will come) to Fukuoka next month.

Answers

1＿＿＿＿＿＿　2＿＿＿＿＿＿　3＿＿＿＿＿＿　4＿＿＿＿＿＿　5＿＿＿＿＿＿

Exercise 2　1と2は［　　］内の語（句）を並べ替え、3〜5は日本文にあう英文を
各々書いてみましょう。　　　　（注：文頭の文字と句読点は、要適宜対応）
1　今日は雨だったので、僕は車を洗わなかった。

[today, wash, because, I, the car, it, didn' t, rained]

➔＿＿＿＿＿＿＿＿＿＿＿＿＿＿＿＿＿＿＿＿＿＿＿＿＿＿＿＿＿＿＿＿＿

2　明日、何が起こるか誰にもわからない。

[will, knows, tomorrow, nobody, what, happen]

➔＿＿＿＿＿＿＿＿＿＿＿＿＿＿＿＿＿＿＿＿＿＿＿＿＿＿＿＿＿＿＿＿＿

3　主人は風邪をひいたので、今日の午後、病院に行くつもりです。

➔＿＿＿＿＿＿＿＿＿＿＿＿＿＿＿＿＿＿＿＿＿＿＿＿＿＿＿＿＿＿＿＿＿

4　警察は誰がその火事を最初に知らせたかを調査すると言っている。

［ヒント：〜を調査する☞ investigate]

➔＿＿＿＿＿＿＿＿＿＿＿＿＿＿＿＿＿＿＿＿＿＿＿＿＿＿＿＿＿＿＿＿＿

5　海外旅行が私の趣味です。去年はヨーロッパ５か国を廻ってきました。今年はハワ
イに行く予定です。　　　　　　　　［ヒント：海外（を）☞ aborad]

➔＿＿＿＿＿＿＿＿＿＿＿＿＿＿＿＿＿＿＿＿＿＿＿＿＿＿＿＿＿＿＿＿＿

16

Coffee Break 3

ダンクシュート

　バスケットボールの魅力の一つにダンクシュートがある。身長２ｍ前後の選手が、ゴールのバスケットにボールを投げるのではなく、その上から直接ボールを持って押し込むシュートは、その選手は勿論、観衆にとっても醍醐味である。

　ところが、今日のような強烈なダンクシュートはバスケットボールの発明当初は、無理であったようだ。バスケットボールが発明された頃は、ゴールは、収穫した桃を入れておく籠が使用されていた。底がある籠。従ってボールは、ゴールの度にその籠から取り出していたが、これだと試合も一時的に中断する。やがて底のないゴールに改良され試合の流れもスムーズになり、今日のようなダンクシュートも可能になった。こうしてバスケットボールの魅力がまた一つ生まれ、その人気アップに寄与した。

photo by All-Pro Reels

Unit 4 Rui's Road to the NBA

I Vocabulary Checking

A 群の英単語の日本語訳を B 群より選びその記号を [　] に記入しなさい。

◆ A 群

1 commit　[　　]　　2 crowds [　　]　　3 congratulate [　　]

4 overcome [　　]　　5 fluent　[　　]

◆ B 群

a ～を克服する　　**b** 真剣に取組む　　**c** 観客　　**d** ～を祝福する　　**e** 流暢な

II Reading

☆ **Before Reading Passage**（Q［質問・指針］を念頭に passage［本文］を読んでみましょう）

Q1 八村 塁とは誰ですか？（生い立ち、名前の由来、学歴等）

Q2 八村 塁のバスケットボールを始めたきっかけから NBA のドラフト指名までの流れを読み取りましょう。

Q3 八村 塁の NBA1 年目はどんな年でしたか？

☆ **Words & Phrases**（単語、語句のヒント）

1 name recognition 知名度　　2 standout 傑出した　　3 grateful 感謝する　　4 stardom スターの地位

☆ **Passage**

　In June 2019, Rui Hachimura made history. The Wizards, the NBA team in Washington D.C., picked Rui Hachimura, a junior forward at Gonzaga University, in the first round of the NBA draft. Rui, 6 feet and 8 inches tall, is the first Japanese player to be selected in the first round of the NBA draft.

　Rui was born in 1998 in Toyama City to a注 1Beninese father and a Japanese mother. His baseball-loving grandfather named him Rui, which translates to "base" in English. On entering junior high school, his interest switched from baseball to basketball after his friend's insistence on giving basketball a try. His junior high school coach Jyoji Sakamoto also told him to try basketball, even to consider playing in the NBA someday. Entering Meisei High School in Sendai and elevating his 1name recognition at home and abroad as a 2standout high school player, Rui drew attention from some U.S. colleges. In 2016, he entered Gonzaga University in Washington State, the first step on his path to the NBA.

　Rui's initial year in Gonzaga, however, was not easy. He had difficulty in adjusting to new circumstances with his limited English and cultural differences. **Overcoming** the hardships, Rui would soon become a star player for the Bulldogs. Impressing the interviewer with his **fluent** English in an interview in the second year, Rui said that to play in the NBA was his goal and he was [3]grateful to coach Sakamoto and his friend in junior high. Soon after the NBA draft, Rui called coach Sakamoto to thank him. His former coach **congratulated** him while sheddding tears of happiness. In an interview after the draft, he replied that his goal in the NBA was to play in the playoffs and to win the championship.

In October 2019, Rui made an impressive NBA debut. He scored 14 points and 10 rebounds in a game against the Dallas Mavericks. In Febuary 2020, Rui impressed the **crowds** and media playing in the Rising Stars game. Rui's rookie year in the NBA ended with a remarkable record, playing as a starter in[注2]48 games and scoring 13.5 on average and taking down an average of 6.1 rebounds a game.

Rui's [4]stardom in the NBA has just started. As he will continue to **commit** to achieving his NBA goal in the years ahead, so will media attention and others' high expectation of his great performance. No doubt among them is coach Sakamoto who guided Rui on the road to the NBA.

注1　Beninese ベナン人　ベナン共和国（Republic of Benin）アフリカ西部にある国
注2　新型コロナ禍の影響でレギュラーシーズンのウイザーズの試合数は72試合。八村は2019年12月16日の試合で負傷し、翌年2月初旬まで24試合を欠場した。

III　Listening Comprehension

Listen to the CD and choose the correct answer about the passage.

1　A　Rui changed his interest from baseball to basketball.

　　B　in Sendai where he made his name well known at home and abroad

　　C　No, Meisei High School is not in Toyama City.

2　A　Hachimura was born in Toyama.

　　B　Rui entered Gonzaga University.

　　C　Hachimura started his professional career in the NBA.

3　A　He played in the Rising Stars game.

　　B　The interviewer was impressed by Rui's natural English.

　　C　He called coach Sakamoto to thank him.

4　A　The NBA team Wizards is not in the state of Washington.

　　B　Hachimura was quite good at English when he entered Gonzaga University.

　　C　Rui started basketball in Meisei senior high school where he met coach Sakamoto.

Answers　1＿＿＿＿＿＿　2＿＿＿＿＿＿　3＿＿＿＿＿＿　4＿＿＿＿＿＿

ハーフタイム

☆ **Philadelphia 76ers**（フィラデルフィア **76ers**）

独立宣言書が作成された独立記念館

　アメリカ東部の都市フィラデルフィアを本拠地にする NBA チーム名。その由来は 1776 年の下 2 桁の 76 年。この年はフィラデルフィアでイギリスの植民地だったアメリカが独立を決定し独立宣言書を作成した歴史的な年だった。1776 年は同都市には特別な年なのである。

Ⅳ Back to Basics（英文法の基礎）④　助動詞

・ポイント 1　助動詞の位置 ☞ 動詞の前に置く。また、続く動詞は常に原形。
・ポイント 2　疑問文 ☞ 助動詞を主語の前に置く。否定文 ☞ 助動詞の後ろに not を置く。
・ポイント 3　助動詞の過去時制　助動詞を過去形に変えるか同義語（句）を過去形にして表す。

助 動 詞	意　　　味	下記例文	同義・類語（句）	過 去 形
can	～できる、～のはずだ（否定が多い）	A	be able to	could
must	～しなければならない、～にちがいない	B	have（has）to	had to
may	～してよい、～かもしれない	C	―	might
will	～でしょう、～するつもり 等＊	D	be going to	would
should	～するべき	E	ought to	―
had better	～しなさい、～したほうがよい	F	―	―

A I can play the piano. ／ His story cannot be true.（cannot: ～のはずがない）
B I must（= have to）finish this work by noon.
C You may use this PC when you want.
D It will be rainy tomorrow. ／ I will（= am going to）major in history at the college.
E You should（= ought to）leave at once.　　F You had better see a doctor.
　注　had better の 否定文 ☞ You had better not touch this machine.

＊ will, would, could は、「お願い」や「誘い」の意味もある。
　Will you do me a favor?（お願いがあるんだけど）
　Would you join us?（ご一緒しませんか？）
　Could you pass me the sugar?　（お砂糖、とってくれませんか）

Exercise 1　次の各英文の（　　）内から最も適当な語（句）を選び、その記号を下の解答欄に記入しなさい。

1 My sister Mary（ア can　イ have to　ウ must　エ should）play the piano better than me.

2（ア May　イ Should　ウ Will　エ Must）I go home? I'm afraid I have a cold.

3 You（ア must　イ had　ウ may　エ should）better study harder.

4 It is cold in this room.（ア Should　イ May　ウ Must　エ Will）you close the window?

5 My son（ア must　イ cannot　ウ should　エ will）be very tired after studying for hours.

Answers

1＿＿＿＿＿＿　2＿＿＿＿＿＿　3＿＿＿＿＿＿　4＿＿＿＿＿＿　5＿＿＿＿＿＿

Exercise 2　1と2は〔　　〕内の語（句）を並べ替え、3〜5は日本文にあう英文を各々書いてみましょう。　　（注：文頭の文字と句読点は、要適宜対応）

1　今日の午後、君の車を貸してもらえないか？

〔use, car, this, your, I, may, afternoon〕

➜＿＿＿＿＿＿＿＿＿＿＿＿＿＿＿＿＿＿＿＿＿＿＿＿＿＿＿＿＿＿＿

2　もう少し大きな声で話していただけませんか。（私は）君の言うことが聞こえません。（2文）　　〔speak, you, can't, your voice, a little, hear, will, louder, I〕

➜＿＿＿＿＿＿＿＿＿＿＿＿＿＿＿＿＿＿＿＿＿＿＿＿＿＿＿＿＿＿＿

3　「我々が旅行で留守中は、ペット（複数）はどうしようか。」「私が世話しますよ。」

➜＿＿＿＿＿＿＿＿＿＿＿＿＿＿＿＿＿＿＿＿＿＿＿＿＿＿＿＿＿＿＿

4　航空機は間もなく離陸します。乗客の皆様はシートベルトを締めなくてはなりません。

➜＿＿＿＿＿＿＿＿＿＿＿＿＿＿＿＿＿＿＿＿＿＿＿＿＿＿＿＿＿＿＿

5　私は市が公園を作るためにその土地を購入すべきだという市長の考えに賛同できない。

➜＿＿＿＿＿＿＿＿＿＿＿＿＿＿＿＿＿＿＿＿＿＿＿＿＿＿＿＿＿＿＿

Coffee Break 4

Madison Square Garden（MSG）
マディソン・スクエアー・ガーデン

　ニューヨーク市マンハッタン地区のほぼ中心にある多目的屋内施設。その歴史は、1879年（明治11年）に始まり、サーカス、ボクシングの試合等が開催された。1964年に現在地に移転し、1968年オープンして今日に至るまで、種々のイベント会場としての場を提供する等ニューヨークの顔の一つである。

　まず20世紀に入り、プロバスケットボールが発展すると、1968年オープンと同時にNBAのNew York Nicksのホームに。NBAのオールスターゲームも複数回開催された。ボクシングでは、あのモハメド・アリの試合が開催された。また、ボブ・ディランを始めローリング・ストーンズ、ボン・ジョビ、エルトン・ジョン等の有名アーチストのコンサートも開催されてきた。その歴史は、アメリカのスポーツや娯楽（entertainment）の変遷と共に歩みその発展の一翼を担ってきたのである。

　2013年、3年がかりの大改造工事を終えて多目的屋内アリーナとしての魅力を益々アップさせたMSG。世界のトップクラスのアーチストやプロスポーツ選手等にとっては、そのコンサートや試合の開催会場として"羨望の的"である。

　場所は、大晦日のカウントダウンで知られるタイムズ・スクエアーからも南西へ数百メートルの徒歩圏内にある。ニューヨークを訪問する機会があれば、自由の女神像訪問、ブロードウェイでのミュージカル観劇、5番街散策に加え、MSGでのNBAの試合観戦も旅程に加えてみてはいかが。

　バスケットボールの試合時の収容人員数は約19,000人。

Unit 5 Football - The Most Popular Sport in the USA

I Vocabulary Checking

A群の英単語の日本語訳をB群より選びその記号を〔　　〕に記入しなさい。

◆A群

1 substitutions　〔　　〕　　2 capacities〔　　〕　　3 allow〔　　〕

4 intercollegiate〔　　〕　　5 merger　〔　　〕

◆B群

a ～を認める　　**b** 大学対抗の　　**c** 合併　　**d** 選手交代　　**e** 能力、収容人数

II Reading

☆ **Before Reading Passage**(Q〔質問・指針〕を念頭に passage〔本文〕を読んでみましょう)

Q1 アメフト（アメリカンフットボール）の起源と、アメリカでの普及について読み取りましょう。

Q2 アメフトと他のスポーツを比較して言えることは何ですか。また、何故ですか。

Q3 NFL の構成やシーズンについて読み取りましょう。

☆ **Words & Phrases**（単語、語句のヒント）

1 advance パスする　2 sideways 横の　3 conquer に広がる　4 demonstrate 示す　5 conferences リーグ

☆ **Passage**

In America, baseball, basketball, and football are the three most popular spectator sports. Of the three, however, football seems to be the one that attracts the most spectators per game. Football was created in America in the late 1860s as an American version of English rugby. While a forward pass is **allow**ed in football in [1]advancing the ball, it is not allowed in rugby. Only [2]sideways and backwards passes are allowed in rugby. Also, **substitutions** are unlimited in football but they are not in rugby.

Football first spread among universities and has been the most popular college sport ever since. The game between Princeton and Rutgers in 1869 is said to be the first **intercollegiate** football game. Harvard and Yale played their first football game in 1875. Before long, football spread to other[注1]**Ivy League** colleges, eight in total and all of which are located in the northeastern part of the nation. In 1880, an intercollegiate football association was created and football would soon [3]conquer many U.S. colleges and universities. Today, most of those American universities with football teams have their own stadiums on campus. Michigan Stadium on the campus of the University of Michigan in Ann Arbor, for example, has seats for about 110,000 fans. Memorial Stadium on the campus of the University of California at Berkeley can seat 71,800 spectators. Their **capacities** well [4]demonstrate the popularity of football in America. Star college players after graduation often continue to play in the professional league, the National Football League (NFL).

The NFL, which was created with the **merger** of [注2]two existing leagues in 1966, now has two [5]conferences, the American Conference and the National Conference. As of 2020, each conference has sixteen teams. The regular season lasts five months starting in September and ending in January. College players look forward to the NFL draft usually held in April. The draft serves as the most common way of recruiting star football players across the nation.

注1　Ivy League（アイビーリーグ）大学。Harvard、Yale、Pennsylvania、Princeton、Brown、Columbia、Dartmouth、Cornell の 8 大学。

注2　the National Football League（NFL）と the American Football League（AFL）

Ⅲ　Listening Comprehension

Listen to the CD and choose the correct answer about the passage.

1　A　The football season starts.

　　B　Two existing professional leagues merged in 1966.

　　C　The NFL draft is held.

2　A　They played the first college football game.

　　B　Yes, they are among the Ivy League universities.

　　C　These two colleges played their first football game.

3　A　Yes, football is the American version of English rugby.

　　B　While a forward pass is allowed in football, it is not in rugby.

　　C　The football season lasts longer than that of rugby.

4　A　The first intercollegiate football game was held in 1875.

　　B　It seems that football is the sport that attracts the most spectators per game.

　　C　The number of seats available at college stadiums well shows the popularity of football.

Answers 1　　　　　　 2　　　　　　 3　　　　　　 4

ハーフタイム

☆ヤード（**yard**）　フットボールやゴルフの距離／長さの基本となる単位

米国で長さを示す主な単位

1 inch　（インチ）・・・ 約 2.5 cm　　1 foot　（フット）・・・ 約 30 cm、

1 yard　（ヤード）・・・ 約 91 cm、　　1 mile　（マイル）・・・ 約 1.6 km

IV　Back to Basics（英文法の基礎）⑤　進行形

・ポイント **1**　ある動作が進行している状態を進行形と言い、英語では "be 動詞＋動詞 ing" で表す。現在進行形、過去進行形、未来進行形等がある。なお、現在進行形は近い未来を表すこともある。

・現在進行形　Ken is washing his car. / It is raining hard now.

I am leaving this evening.（近い未来）

・過去進行形　Ken was washing his car at the gas station.

Where were you washing your car?

・未来進行形　He will be washing his car this afternoon.

What will he be doing at this time tomorrow?

・ポイント **2**　所有、状態などを表す動詞は進行形にはしない。

（○）I have many books.　　　　　　（×）I am having many books.

注：I am having lunch now. は可。ここの have は「食べる」の意味。

（○）I like cats.　　　　　　　　　（×）I am liking cats.

（○）Do you know that man?　　　　（×）Are you knowing that man?

・ポイント **3**　動詞 ing の作り方（つづり）で注意を要する単語。

・基本　動詞の原形に ing を追加する。ただし、下記のようなつづりの単語は要注意。

つづりの最後が e や ie の単語　例：come ☞ coming、live ☞ living、lie ☞ lying 等

・短母音＋子音字の単語は、原則、子音字を重ねてから ing 例：run ☞ running、swim ☞ swimming 等

Exercise 1　次の各英文の（　　）内から適当な語（句）を選び、その記号を下の解答欄に記入しなさい。

1 Tom and I （ア am study　イ are studying　ウ were studying　エ be studying） English now.

2 Tom is （ア takeing　イ takes　ウ being take　エ taking） a picture of my sister.

3 My brother （ア having　イ is having　ウ has　エ being has） many CDs.

4 What were you （ア looked　イ be looking　ウ look　エ looking） at there?

5 I （ア know　イ am knowing　ウ knowing　エ am know） some French words.

Answers

1＿＿＿＿＿＿　2＿＿＿＿＿＿　3＿＿＿＿＿＿　4＿＿＿＿＿＿　5＿＿＿＿＿＿

Exercise 2　1と2は〔　　〕内の語（句）を並べ替え、3〜5は日本文にあう英文を各々書いてみましょう。　　　　　（注：文頭の文字と句読点は、要適宜対応）

1　母は今、台所で夕食の準備をしています。

〔in, is, the, my, cooking, kitchen, now, dinner, mother〕

→＿＿＿＿＿＿＿＿＿＿＿＿＿＿＿＿＿＿＿＿＿＿＿＿＿＿＿＿＿＿

2　その老人が犬を散歩させている間、僕達は公園でサッカーをしていた。

We 〔playing, walking, the old, while, in the park, his dog, was, soccer, were〕

→　We＿＿＿＿＿＿＿＿＿＿＿＿＿＿＿＿＿＿＿＿＿＿＿＿＿＿

3　父は雨が激しく降っていたので、その時はゆっくり運転していた。

→＿＿＿＿＿＿＿＿＿＿＿＿＿＿＿＿＿＿＿＿＿＿＿＿＿＿＿＿＿＿

4　僕が二階の部屋で勉強している間、僕の兄弟はリビングでテレビを見ていた。

→＿＿＿＿＿＿＿＿＿＿＿＿＿＿＿＿＿＿＿＿＿＿＿＿＿＿＿＿＿＿

5　今、市役所の近くに新しい公立図書館が建設中で、来春の完成を皆、心待ちにしています。　　　　　　　　　　　〔ヒント：完成 ☞ completion〕

→＿＿＿＿＿＿＿＿＿＿＿＿＿＿＿＿＿＿＿＿＿＿＿＿＿＿＿＿＿＿

Coffee Break 5

アメリカの車等の速度はマイル表示

　市街地など一般道路の速度制限（Speed Limit）は普通 25mile（約 40km）。郊外では 45mile（約 75km）、高速道路では 55mile（約 90km）〜 60mile（約 100km）が多いようだ。

ハワイ州の都市郊外の速度制限道路標識

Unit 6 Super Bowl

Ⅰ   Vocabulary Checking

A 群の英単語の日本語訳を B 群より選びその記号を［　　］に記入しなさい。

◆ A 群

1 broadcast ［　　］　　2 last　　　　［　　］　　3 viewers　　［　　］

4 pastime(s)［　　］　　5 proceed　［　　］

◆ B 群

a 続く　　**b** 観衆　　**c** 放送する　　**d** 進む　　**e** 娯楽

Ⅱ   Reading

CD
12

☆ **Before Reading Passage**（Q［質問・指針］を念頭に passage［本文］を読んでみましょう）

Q1 スーパーボウルとは何のことですか（名前の由来、いつ開催、選手や国民の関心度等）？

Q2 NFL のシーズンはいつですか（開始～終了）？また、一試合の流れは？

Q3 ハーフ・タイム・ショウとは？（その役割、過去の登場人物等）

☆ **Words & Phrases**（単語、語句のヒント）

1 annual 例年の　　　2 founder 創設者　　　3 consist of ～から成る　　　4 survive 勝ち残る　　　5 bored 退屈に

☆ **Passage**

The Super Bowl is America's most watched [1]annual sporting event. The
championship game is usually held in early February. The game is **broadcast** live on
television as well as on the Internet and excites tens of millions of **viewers** as well as
live spectators at the stadium. The number of TV viewers from 1990 to 2020 varied
roughly between 74 million and 114 million.

The championship game was called the AFL-NFL World Championship Game in
the first two years in 1967 and 1968. Since 1969 they started to call it the Super Bowl.
It owes its naming to Lamar Hunt, the [2]founder of the American Football League and
the owner of the NFL's Kansas City Chiefs. Mr. Hunt hit upon the name when he
saw his daughter playing with a toy called Super Ball, not[注]bowl.

Winning the the Super Bowl is the goal of every NFL player. The NFL regular
season usually starts early in September and ends late in December. The playoff
games are held in January the next year. Each team plays sixteen games a year, one
game a week, usually on Sundays. One game [3]consists of four quarters and usually

lasts about two hours including the halftime. Watching a Sunday football game on TV is one of the favorite **pastimes** among many Americans. The top team which ⁴survives the playoffs in each conference at the end of the season **proceeds** to the Super Bowl.

If the Super Bowl is the biggest sporting event in the USA, the halftime show is another highlight of the event to fill the halftime and entertain fans. The crowds and TV viewers never get ⁵bored during the halftime break while watching great performances by superstars. Among them were Michael Jackson in 1993, Paul McCartney in 2005, Lady Gaga in 2017, and Jennifer Lopez and Shakira in 2020, to name a few.

As of 2020, the New England Patriots and the Pittsburgh Steelers have won the most Super Bowl titles, six each of the more than 50 Super Bowl games. The Super Bowl will likely continue to be the most popular sporting event in the United States.

注　bowl スタジアムがお椀（bowl）の形に似ているのが語源という説がある。

Ⅲ　Listening Comprehension

Listen to the CD and choose the correct answer about the passage.

1　A　Michael Jackson performed during the halftime show in 1993.

　　B　Yes, many Americans watch the game on TV as well as on the Internet.

　　C　It is a championship game of professional football in America.

2　A　One game consists of four quarters but lasts about two hours including the halftime.

　　B　It starts in the late summer.

　　C　It started in 1967.

3　A　Yes, each team in the NFL plays sixteen games a year, one game a week.

　　B　It is one of the favorite pastimes among the many Americans.

　　C　It is not clear from the passage.

4　A　The Super Bowl is a game played by star players selected by voting of the fans.

　　B　The NFL season lasts about five months, starting in the late summer.

　　C　The halftime show is helpful not to make the crowds and TV viewers get bored.

Answers　1＿＿＿＿＿＿＿＿＿　2＿＿＿＿＿＿＿＿＿　3＿＿＿＿＿＿＿＿＿　4＿＿＿＿＿＿＿＿＿

ハーフタイム

"☆**The 49ers**" サンフランシスコを本拠地とする NFL プロフットボールチーム名。

この名は、1849 年の下 2 桁に由来する。1848 年、サンフランシスコ近郊で金の鉱脈が発見された翌年、アメリカ国内外から一攫千金を求めてこの地に多くの人達が押し寄せた。

名物ケーブルカー

ゴールドラッシュである。その後の同都市の発展に大きく寄与した。

サンフランシスコ

アメリカ西海岸を代表する都市。テレビ番組 "フルハウス" の舞台。金門橋、チャイナタウン等で有名。

IV Back to Basics（英文法の基礎）⑥ 受動態

英語の動詞には、他動詞（目的語「(訳すと)〜を、に」を伴う動詞）と自動詞（目的語を伴わない動詞）がある。

・ポイント **1**　他動詞を含む文を「〜する」等と訳す場合は能動態と言い、「〜される」と訳す場合は受動態と言う。

　　　　　　　この受動態の英語の基本形は、"**be 動詞 ＋ 過去分詞 ＋ by（等）・・・**"で表す。

　例　Everyone loves Sue. ☞ Sue <u>is loved by</u> everyone. / He wrote this letter. ☞ This letter <u>was written by</u> him.

・ポイント **2**　動詞により 'by' 以外の語を使用する場合がある。

　例　He is known to everyone in the town.　[be known to 〜：〜に知られている]

　　　The street was covered with snow this morning. [be covered with 〜：〜で覆われている]

　　　This desk is made of wood. / Butter is made from milk. [be made of（材料）/ from（原料）〜：〜できている]

・ポイント **3**　人間の感情等を表す「〜する、である」も受動態を使って表すことがある。

　例　We **are surprised at** the news.　　　[be surprised at 〜：〜に驚く]

　　　Mary **is pleased with** her new coat.　[be pleased with 〜：〜を喜ぶ]

　　　Are you **interested in** this book?　　[be interested in 〜：〜に興味を持つ]

　　　I **am tired of** my work. [be tired of 〜：〜に飽きる]/ I am tired with my work.

　　　　　　　　　　　　[be tired with 〜：〜に疲れる]

Exercise 1　次の各英文の（　　）内から適当な語（句）を選び、その記号を下の解答欄に記入しなさい。

1 The photo（ア was taken　イ took　ウ is taking　エ be taken）by my brother.

2 America（ア is discovered　イ was discovered　ウ discovered　エ was discovering）by Columbus.

3 The sky is（ア covered at　イ covering by　ウ covered by　エ covered with）clouds.

4 I was（ア surprising at　イ surprised by　ウ surprised at　エ surprising by）the scene.

5 Is your son interested（ア by　イ with　ウ at　エ in）baseball?

Answers

1＿＿＿＿＿＿　2＿＿＿＿＿＿　3＿＿＿＿＿＿　4＿＿＿＿＿＿　5＿＿＿＿＿＿

Exercise 2　1と2は［　　］内の語（句）を並べ替え、3〜5は日本文にあう英文を各々書いてみましょう。　　（注：文頭の文字と句読点は、要適宜対応）

1　この美しい写真は君の兄が撮ったのですか。

[taken, this, by, photo, your brother, beautiful, was]

➔＿＿＿＿＿＿＿＿＿＿＿＿＿＿＿＿＿＿＿＿＿＿＿＿＿＿＿＿

2　私は娘がサッカーに関心があると聞いて驚いています。

[in, am, interested, our daughter, I, soccer, is, to hear, that, surprised]

➔＿＿＿＿＿＿＿＿＿＿＿＿＿＿＿＿＿＿＿＿＿＿＿＿＿＿＿＿

3　僕はその車にはねられた直後に、この病院に搬送された。

［ヒント：直後☞ soon after, 搬送する ☞ take］

➔＿＿＿＿＿＿＿＿＿＿＿＿＿＿＿＿＿＿＿＿＿＿＿＿＿＿＿＿

4　彼の両親は息子がその NBA のチームに選ばれたというニュースに喜んだ。

［ヒント：〜を喜ばす☞ please、〜を選ぶ ☞ select］

➔＿＿＿＿＿＿＿＿＿＿＿＿＿＿＿＿＿＿＿＿＿＿＿＿＿＿＿＿

5　今月末までには、その会社の新車が発売されるということだ（と言われている）。

［ヒント： 発売する ☞ put on sale］

➔＿＿＿＿＿＿＿＿＿＿＿＿＿＿＿＿＿＿＿＿＿＿＿＿＿＿＿＿

Coffee Break 6

スーパーボウルのハーフタイムに登場したアーチスト

2000 年　Enrique Iglesias（スペインの大御所フリオ・イグレシアスの息子）
2001 年　Aerosmith, Britney Spears
2002 年　U2
2006 年　The Rolling Stones
2007 年　Prince
2009 年　Bruce Springsteen
2012 年　Madonna
2019 年　Maroon 5, Travis Scott

1988 年シーズン、サンフランシスコ 49ers のスーパーボウル優勝を祝う市民。（1989 年 2 月、サンフランシスコ中心街マーケット通り）

Unit 7 Wimbledon

I Vocabulary Checking

A群の英単語の日本語訳をB群より選びその記号を［　　］に記入しなさい。

- ◆ A群

  1 spectators ［　　］   2 strict   ［　　］   3 interruption ［　　］

  4 surface   ［　　］   5 compete   ［　　］

- ◆ B群

  a 中断、邪魔   **b** 観客   **c** 厳格な   **d** 競う、プレーする   **e** 表面

II Reading

☆ **Before Reading Passage**(Q［質問・指針］を念頭に passage［本文］を読んでみましょう。)

Q1 テニスの4大大会の一つウィンブルドン選手権と他の4大大会権と違う点とそのメリットは何でしょうか？

Q2 伝統を重んじるウィンブルドンが2009年に取り入れたことと、その理由は何でしょうか？

Q3 **Andrew B. Murray** 選手は何故、注目されたのですか？

☆ **Words & Phrases** （単語、語句のヒント）

1 cherish 大事にする   2 competitor 選手   3 retractable 可動式の   4 witness 見る   5 male 男性

☆ **Passage**

Today, there are four major tennis tournaments held annually in the world. They are the Championships, Wimbledon, held in early summer in London, the French Open, the U.S. Open, and the Australian Open. Although the Australian Open and the French Open are held before Wimbledon in the calendar year, Wimbledon has the longest history of all. Wimbledon lasts for two weeks at the beginning of July.

Starting in the late 1870s, Wimbledon has [1]cherished its tradition. For example, it has always been played on grass courts, the only major tournament that is played on this surface. Grass courts are said to produce irregular bounces to the ball because of the softer and unsmooth **surface** of grass. This feature of the grass court serves as an advantage for players with good serves. Wimbledon also keeps a **strict** dress code for [2]competitors who have to wear white uniforms.

While keeping to traditions, the home to Wimbledon has made some changes. In April 2009, a [3]retractable roof was installed over Center Court so that there would be no long delays or **interruptions** due to rain. It has been a dream for many professional tennis players to **compete** in Wimbledon, especially on Center Court. Along with **spectators**, the court has [4]witnessed legendary stars, such as Jimmy Connors, Ivan Lendl, and Boris Becker among the men as well as Chris Evert, Martina Navratilova, and Steffi Graf among the women. Navratilova has won the most titles with nine in all.

Although it is held in the U.K., few British players have won championships at Wimbledon. It was in 2013 that Andrew B. Murray beat Novak Djokovic and became the first British [5]male player in 77 years to win a Grand Slam singles tournament since Fred Perry in 1936. Winning another major tournament and a gold medal in the Rio De Janeiro Olympics in 2016, Murray was ranked number one in the world in November 2016. The last British women's winner of Wimbledon championship was Virginia Wade in 1977.

III   Listening Comprehension

Listen to the CD and choose the correct answer about the passage.

1   A   in spring

   B   It started in the late 1870s.

   C   in early summer

2   A   She is a legendary star tennis player.

   B   She won the Wimbledon championship in 1977.

   C   Ms. Graf won four major tennis tournaments in 2009.

3   A   A British female player won the Championships for the first time.

   B   They built a new roof over Center Court.

   C   No game was cancelled because of rain.

4   A   The U.S. Open and Wimbledon are held after the Australia Open every year.

   B   As of 2020, Andrew B. Murray has won Wimbledon once.

   C   Only Wimbledon of the four major tournaments is played on grass courts.

Answers 1 _____   2 _____   3 _____   4 _____

ハーフタイム

☆コーチとして活躍するかつてのグランドスラム優勝スター選手

◆ Ivan Lendl（チェコスロバキア［現チェコ］）➡ Andrew B. Murray のコーチ
  ・グランドスラム優勝回数8回（全て1980年代）濠2回、仏3回、米3回、ウインブルドンは準優勝2回。

◆ Michael Chang（台湾系アメリカ人）➡ 錦織 圭のコーチ
  ・グランドスラム優勝1回　全仏［1989年］、準優勝2回—豪［1996年］、米［1996年］。

IV　Back to Basics（英文法の基礎）⑦　現在完了形

現在完了形 ☞ 過去に始まったある行動や状態が、現在を中心に何らかの影響がある場合等に使う。

・ポイント 1 現在完了形の英語の基本形 ➡ have（又は has）＋ 過去分詞 (pp)
・ポイント 2 完了、結果、経験、継続の用法・意味がある。（下記例文 A ～ D）
・ポイント 3 疑問文 ➡ have / has を主語の前に置く（下記 C）。
　　　　　　否定文 ➡ have / has の後に not や never。

A　I have done my homework.（完了）　　B　She has lost her bag.（結果）

C　Have you ever visited Hawaii?（経験）　D　Tom has lived in Japan for ten years.（継続）

・ポイント 4 現在完了形は、過去を表わす語（句）とは一緒には使わない。☞下記例文 E 左の文
　　　　　　ただし「since + 過去の語（句）」は例外。　☞下記例文 E 右の文

また、When が「いつ」という意味の場合は、現在完了形とは一緒には使わない。
（下記例文 F）

E　I have done my homework yesterday.（×）/ My son has been sick since last night.（○）

F　When have you done your homework?（×）/ When did you do your homework?（○）

Exercise 1　次の各英文の（　　）内から適当な語（句）を選び、その記号を下の解答欄に記入しなさい。

1 I（ア have lost　イ was lost　ウ losed　エ was losing）the watch my father gave me.

2 Mary（ア has cooked　イ have cooked　ウ was cooked　エ done cooking）dinner.

3 Ten years（ア have been　イ did passed　ウ were passed　エ have passed）since the actor died.

4 The famous musician（ア has died　イ dead　ウ has dead　エ died）last year.

5 When（ア have you　イ did you　ウ were you　エ have you been）see the UFO?

6 If you（ア have been done　イ did　ウ have done　エ will do）your work, you may go out to play soccer.

Answers

1＿＿＿＿＿　2＿＿＿＿＿　3＿＿＿＿＿　4＿＿＿＿＿　5＿＿＿＿＿　6＿＿＿＿＿

Exercise 2　1と2は［　　］内の語（句）を並べ替え、3～5は日本文にあう英文を
各々書いてみましょう。　　　（注：文頭の文字と句読点は、要適宜対応）

1　祖母は一週間、病気で寝ています。

[been, for, in bed, a week, has, sick, my grandma]

➔＿＿＿＿＿＿＿＿＿＿＿＿＿＿＿＿＿＿＿＿＿＿＿＿＿＿＿

2　「アメリカを訪問したことがありますか？」「いいえ、ありません。」

[ever, have, visited, you, haven't, America, no, I]

➔＿＿＿＿＿＿＿＿＿＿＿＿＿＿＿＿＿＿＿＿＿＿＿＿＿＿＿

3　「何処に行ってたの？」「（私は）空港に姉を見送りに行ってきたところです。」
［ヒント：～に行ってきた☞ go (gone) ではなく be を使う、人を見送る ☞ see 人 off］

➔＿＿＿＿＿＿＿＿＿＿＿＿＿＿＿＿＿＿＿＿＿＿＿＿＿＿＿

4　ビルと花子は 2010 年にその大学で会って以来の知り合いです。

➔＿＿＿＿＿＿＿＿＿＿＿＿＿＿＿＿＿＿＿＿＿＿＿＿＿＿＿

5　日本の人口は、少子化が原因で減少し始めた。
［ヒント：減少する ☞ decrease、少子化 ☞ low birth rate］

➔＿＿＿＿＿＿＿＿＿＿＿＿＿＿＿＿＿＿＿＿＿＿＿＿＿＿＿

Coffee Break 7

Wimbledon 記録

☆ 男子シングルス最多優勝者　　Roger Federer（スイス）

　　　　　　　　　　　　　　　　2003 年から 2017 年にかけて 8 回

☆ 女子シングルス最多優勝者　　Martina Navratilova（アメリカ）

　　　　　　　　　　　　　　　　1978 年から 1990 年にかけて 9 回

☆ 男子シングルス最年少優勝者　Boris Becker（旧西ドイツ）

　　　　　　　　　　　　　　　　1985 年　17 歳 227 日

☆ 女子シングルス最年少優勝者　Lottie Dod（イギリス）

　　　　　　　　　　　　　　　　1887 年　15 歳 285 日

　　　　　　　　　　　　　　　　　　　　　（2020 年現在）

photo by si.robi

Unit 8　Naomi Osaka - Love

I　Vocabulary Checking

A群の英単語の日本語訳をB群より選びその記号を［　　］に記入しなさい。

◆A群

1 forceful 　　　　［　　］　　2 defeat　［　　］　　3 guidance　［　　］

4 consciousness　［　　］　　5 climb　［　　］

◆B群

a 指導　　**b** 強力な　　**c** 登る　　**d** ～を負かす、～に勝つ　　**e** 意識

II　Reading

☆ **Before Reading Passage**(Q［質問・指針］を念頭に passage［本文］を読んでみましょう)

Q1 大坂なおみの家族構成と居住地の変遷について読み取りましょう。

Q2 大坂なおみが女子テニスで世界50位以内にランクされるまでの流れを読み取りましょう。

Q3 2019年は大坂なおみにとってどんな1年でしたか。

☆ **Words & Phrases**（単語、語句のヒント）

1 inspire 刺激する　　2 dominance 支配　　3 nurture 育てる　　4 pinnacle 頂点　　5 residence 住居

☆ **Passage**

Naomi Osaka is one of the most exciting and talented tennis players in recent years. She was ranked the number one singles player by the Women's Tennis Association (WTA), and she was the first Asian Japanese player to hold that top world ranking.

Osaka was born in October 1997 in Osaka, Japan to a[注1]Haitian father and a Japanese mother. Her mother's family came from Hokkaido. Naomi's grandparents were not happy about Naomi's mother marrying her father. When Naomi was three years old, the family moved to the U.S. They lived with her father's family on Long Island in New York.

Along with her older sister Mari, Naomi started training under their father's **guidance**. Although he had little experience playing tennis, he was [1]inspired to train his daughters in the sport by the success of the Williams sisters, Venus and Serena. The Williams sisters' [2]dominance in professional tennis made him think it was possible to [3]nurture Mari and Naomi the same way. Her family then moved to Florida when she was about nine years old. Naomi improved with training by other coaches, and by the time she was 16 years old, she managed to rise in the rankings to among the top 150 professional women's tennis players in the world. A year later in 2016, she was in the top 50 players in the world.

To talk about her playing style, she is one of the most powerful hitters in women's tennis. Her serve has been clocked at 200 km/h making her among the 10 fastest servers in WTA history. She is also a **forceful** baseline player.

After a couple of years of hard work and focus, Naomi **climb**ed into the number four position in women's professional tennis. Then, at the end of the 2018 season, she exploded into tennis fans' **consciousness**. Osaka won three Grand Slam singles tournaments, first the U.S. Open **defeat**ing her idol Serena Williams, and then in 2019 she came out on top at the Australian Open. Naomi Osaka finally reached the [4]pinnacle of the WTA number one player in the world in 2019. And in September 2020, Osaka won her second US Open title. In the championship match, she demonstrated her physical and mental growth by winning the last two sets after losing decidedly the first set.

As she is still a young player, Naomi's future looks bright. In 2019, she chose [注2]Japanese citizenship despite her main [5]**residence** in Florida. Many Japanese love Naomi speaking shyly but humorously in her improving Japanese. She is the pride of her family, her fans, and the people of Japan. We wish her the best and cheer her on.

注1　Haitian ハイチ人 Haiti は中央アメリカの西インド諸島にある共和国。
注2　2019 年の誕生日時、日米の二重国籍から日本国籍を選択した。

Ⅲ　Listening Comprehension

Listen to the CD and choose the correct answer about the passage.

1　A　Naomi's mother came to Osaka from Hokkaido in 1977.

　　B　in 1997 in Osaka, Japan

　　C　Naoimi'f family moved to New York when she was three.

2　A　Because her father thought Naomi could have training with the Williams sisters there.

　　B　She found her new coaches there.

　　C　It is not clear from the passage.

3　A　Naomi was ranked in the top 50 professional female tennis players in the world.

　　B　Naomi's serve reached 200km/h.

　　C　Naomi Osaka won the U.S. Open, defeating Serena Williams.

4 A Naomi won two Grand Slam singles tournaments in 2019.

    B Naomi was born in Osaka but has lived mostly in America since 2000.

    C Mari, Naomi's older sister, also received some advice about tennis from their father.

Answers   1 _____   2 _____   3 _____   4 _____

ハーフタイム

国際テニス殿堂入り資格クリア

　大坂なおみは、2020 年全米オープン女子シングルで優勝した結果、グランドスラム 3 大会優勝で国際テニス殿堂入りの資格を得た。ただ、実際の殿堂入りは現役引退後の 5 年後以降のことで、随分と先のことである。

　以下は 1970 年代〜 1990 年代に活躍し現役引退後に殿堂入りした名選手。

・男子　ビョルン・ボルグ（1987 年）、ジミー・コナーズ（1998）、ボリス・ベッカー（2003）ら。

・女子　クリス・エバート（1995）、マルチナ・ナブラチロワ（2000）、シュテフィ・グラフ（2004）ら。

Ⅳ　Back to Basics（英文法の基礎）⑧　不定詞

・**ポイント 1** "**to + 動詞の原形**" を不定詞と言う。下記のような用法、意味がある。

<u>用　法</u>　　<u>意　味</u>　　<u>例　文</u>

① 名詞的用法・・・（〜する）こと・・・<u>To see</u> is <u>to believe</u>. / My hobby is <u>to play</u> golf.

② 形容詞的用法・・・〜のための・・・Give me something <u>to drink</u>. / I need a pen <u>to write</u> with.

③ 副詞的用法・・・〜するために・・・Tom came here <u>to learn</u> Japanese. / 〜して I am glad <u>to meet</u> you.

・**ポイント 2** 不定詞の前に来る動詞が see, hear, help, let, make（させる、の意味）等の場合は、不定詞の 'to' は省略され原形動詞のみを使う　☞　原形不定詞

    a. I often <u>hear</u> Mary (to) sing in her room.

    b. I <u>saw</u> Tom (to) cross the street.

    c. Please <u>help</u> me (to) carry this big bag. （* to は残しても可）。

    d. The teacher <u>made</u> us (to) change the plan. （made ➜ 〜させた）

    e. <u>Let</u> it (to) be.

Exercise 1　次の各英文の（　　）内から適当な語（句）を選び、その記号を下の解答欄に記入しなさい。

1 Tom left early（ア catch　イ to riding　ウ to catch　エ caught）the bus.

2 I don't know how（ア to play　イ to playing　ウ play　エ be playing）golf.

3 I saw Mary（ア jogged　イ jog　ウ being jogged　エ to jog）in the park.

4 Will you help me（ア to moved　イ move　ウ moving　エ be moved）this big box?

5 It is kind of you（ア to show　イ to teach　ウ tell　エ showing）me the way to the station.

Answers

1＿＿＿＿＿＿　2＿＿＿＿＿＿　3＿＿＿＿＿＿　4＿＿＿＿＿＿　5＿＿＿＿＿＿

Exercise 2　1と2は［　　］内の語（句）を並べ替え、3～5は日本文にあう英文を各々書いてみましょう。　　　（注：文頭の文字と句読点は、要適宜対応）

1　私達はその知らせを聞いて非常に喜びました。

［were, the news, happy, hear, we, to, very］

➔＿＿＿＿＿＿＿＿＿＿＿＿＿＿＿＿＿＿＿＿＿＿＿＿＿＿＿＿

2　トムはマリアに電話しようかどうかわからなかった。

［call, did, Maria, not, know, Tom, whether, or, to］

➔＿＿＿＿＿＿＿＿＿＿＿＿＿＿＿＿＿＿＿＿＿＿＿＿＿＿＿＿

3　その試験に合格するのは難しい。先生は我々に毎日勉強するように言っている。

➔＿＿＿＿＿＿＿＿＿＿＿＿＿＿＿＿＿＿＿＿＿＿＿＿＿＿＿＿

4　兄は、私に机の上の彼のパソコンに触れないように言った。

➔＿＿＿＿＿＿＿＿＿＿＿＿＿＿＿＿＿＿＿＿＿＿＿＿＿＿＿＿

5　この夏、ロンドンを訪問する機会があれば遠慮なく我が家にも立ち寄ってください。

［ヒント：立ち寄る ☞ stop by］

➔＿＿＿＿＿＿＿＿＿＿＿＿＿＿＿＿＿＿＿＿＿＿＿＿＿＿＿＿

Coffee Break 8

７枚のマスク

　2020年夏、テニスの全米オープンは、黒人差別を非難するBLM(Black Lives Matter) という抗議運動が全米各地で起こっている最中に開催された。各地で白人警官らによる黒人への暴行死や銃撃事件等が続いていたのである。

　父親が黒人の大坂なおみも、この全米オープン大会で自らの人種差別への抗議の意思を明確に行動で示した。毎試合、犠牲になった黒人の名前をプリントした７枚の黒マスクを着用してコートに入場。マスクの「黒」色にもその意志が反映されているようだった。大坂の望みは、より多くの人が人種差別について語るきっかけになって欲しい、というものだった。

　国籍、性別、人種や民族、宗教・宗派等の差異を問わず公平で公正さの下でアスリートが競いあうスポーツの世界。しばしば言われるスポーツに政治を持ち込むな、との批判には、大坂は、政治対応は十分ですかと問いかけ、他の方法で、と冷めた見方をする者には、傍観を決め込まず具体的行動を呼びかけたのであろう。大坂の非差別から反差別への意識醸成、更には行動への変化の期待を込めたメッセージは重い。

　「これは人権問題」と大坂も言うように、差別への抗議は、「平和」と同様に「平等」という人類普遍の価値観の追求なのである。人種差別に抗議する彼女の姿勢は、スポーツ界だけでなく世界中で注目され、多くの人の共感を呼び、人種を含む種々の差別への問題意識を一層広め、高めたことは間違いない。米国の前オバマ大統領のミッシェル夫人は「誇りに思う。」とツイート。スポーツと政治・宗教・人種問題の分離を規定するIOC憲章の条項の見直し議論も加速しそうだ。

　新型コロナ禍の下、無観客で開催された2020年テニスの全米オープン。大坂のグランドスラム優勝と７枚のマスクに込められた差別への抗議の姿勢は、本来なら観客からスタンディング・オーベションで称えられたことであろう。

　テニスを愛する大坂なおみ。人を平等に愛する大坂なおみ。そんな大坂なおみを見た2020年全米オープンだった。

Unit 9 Tiger Woods' Legend Goes On

photo by Keith Allison

I Vocabulary Checking

A群の英単語の日本語訳をB群より選びその記号を［　　］に記入しなさい。

◆A群

1 turn 　　［　　］ 　　2 inspire 　　［　　］ 　　3 revival 　　　［　　　］

4 suspend 　［　　］ 　　5 turbulent 　［　　］

◆B群

a 中断する 　　**b** 復活 　　**c** 刺激になる、勇気づける 　　**d** 波乱の 　　**e** 転向する

II Reading

CD
○
18

☆ **Before Reading Passage**（Q［質問・指針］を念頭に passage［本文］を読んでみましょう）

Q1 プロゴルファーのタイガー・ウッズの生い立ち～プロ転向までのゴルフ歴をまとめてみましょう。

Q2 プロゴルファーとしてのタイガー・ウッズの世界記録には、どのようなものがありますか。

Q3 タイガー・ウッズのゴルフ活動の一時停止の理由と復帰後、今日までの歩みについて読み取りましょう。

☆ **Words & Phrases**（単語、語句のヒント）

1 prodigy 天才 　　2 mentor 師匠 　　3 revelation 表面化 　　4 infidelity 不貞、不倫 　　5 arrest 逮捕

☆ **Passage**

Tiger Woods is the greatest professional golfer of his generation. He was born in 1975 in Cypress near Los Angeles, California. Earl Woods, Tiger's father, was an amateur golfer and taught him in his early childhood how to play golf. Tiger's talent in golf developed quickly and he became a ¹prodigy by the age of eight. At the age of 12, Tiger defeated his ²mentor, his father. In 1994, Tiger attended Stanford University with a golf scholarship. While a student, he won many amateur tournaments, such as the NCAA individual golf Champion in 1996.

Tiger left college after two years and **turn**ed professional in 1996 at the age of 20. The next year, he won The Masters Golf Tournament in Augusta, USA with a record low score of 270. He was the youngest player ever to win this tournament, which made Tiger famous worldwide. The PGA ranked him number one, the youngest golfer ever to reach that mark. Since then, Woods has won many major tournaments, such as three more U.S. Masters titles. In 2008, he won the U.S. Open, his 14th major victory. Tiger Woods was the number one professional golfer in the world for more weeks than any other player in history. Having won sponsorships with several companies such as Nike and AT&T, Tiger became the world's highest-paid athlete.

Woods would have a **turbulent** decade to come. In 2009, a car accident and [3]revelation of [4]infidelity forced him to **suspend** his career for several months. His struggle continued despite his comeback in 2010 and a win in the Arnold Palmer Invitational Tournament in 2012. Due to several back operations and injuries in the coming years and an [5]arrest for drunk driving in 2017, he could barely play in 2016 and 2017. Woods dropped out of the top 100 players in the world between 2015 and 2017. In April 2019, Woods made an impressive comeback. He won The Masters, his 15th major title but his first in eleven years. His world ranking jumped to sixth place. Several months later in Japan, Tiger showed his real **revival** before Japanese fans and the media by winning in the ZOZO golf tournament. By this vicory, he tied the PGA tournament win record of 82.

Tiger Woods remains one of the most noted professional athletes of all time. He will continue to attract and **inspire** young golfers across the globe.

III Listening Comprehension

Listen to the CD and choose the correct answer about the passage.

1 A His father did.

    B The famous golfer, Arnold Palmer did.

    C Yes, Tiger learned golf at Stanford University.

2 A in 1994

    B in 1996, at the age of twenty

    C He won many amateur tournaments while a student.

3 A He won The Masters title in 1997.

    B Yes, Tiger was ranked number one in 1997.

    C fifteen titles

4 A to finish his studies at Stanford University

    B He had some problems in his private life.

    C He had a car accident and had to have operations on his back.

Answers 1＿＿＿＿＿＿ 2＿＿＿＿＿＿ 3＿＿＿＿＿＿ 4＿＿＿＿＿＿

ハーフタイム

☆ゴルフの起源☆

・諸説あるが、14 世紀、イギリスのスコットランドの羊飼いの遊びが起源と言われる。

15 世紀になると、スコットランドのセントアンドリュース大学の学生に普及。

1750 年代（江戸時代中期）にルール作りがすすむ。英国の植民地を通して世界各地へ普及。

・1860 年 全英オープン、1895 年全米オープン始まる。

・1916 年 プロゴルフ（PGA）発足。プロゴルファーの誕生、活躍、注目に弾みがつく。

・1955 年 女子 PGA 発足。ゴルフも名実共に国境も性別も不問のスポーツの仲間入りを果たす。

IV Back to Basics（英文法の基礎）⑨ 比較1

比　較　☞　人や物等を他のそれらと比較する時の表現。

・**ポイント 1** 英語の形容詞、副詞の中には原級、比較級、最上級の３つの級に変化する
　　　　　　　ものがある。その変化は規則性のあるものと不規則に変化するものがある。

　　・形容詞や副詞　　　　原　級　　　比 較 級　　　　　　最 上 級
　［変化に規則性がある単語］

　・短い　／速い（く）・・・short / fast　shorter / faster　　shortest / fastest
　・易しい／暑い　・・・easy / hot　easier　/ hotter　　easiest / hottest
　・有名な／役立つ・・・famous / useful　more famous / more useful　most famous / most useful

　［変化が不規則な単語］

　・良い（良く）／悪い・・good (well)/ bad　better / worse　best / worst
　・多い　／　少ない・・・many / little　　more　/　less　　most / least

　・文　　章

「同じ～☞ as ～ as」、「より～☞ 比較級の語（句）+ than」、「一番～ ☞ the + 最上級の
語（句）」

　・原　級　Tom is as tall as Bill.　　　　　This watch is as good as that one (= watch).
　・比較級　Tom is taller than Bill.　　　　This watch is better than that one.
　・最上級　Tom is the tallest boy in his class.　This watch is the best of all.

・**ポイント 2** 形容詞の最上級の前には the がつくが、副詞の最上級の前には the はつか
　　　　　　　ない場合も多い。

　　　　　　例　Tom is the fastest runner in his class.
　　　　　　　（この文の fast は形容詞 ☞ 最上級 fastest の前に the が必要）。
　　　　　　　Tom can run (the) fastest in his class.
　　　　　　　（この文の fast は副詞 ☞ 最上級でもその前に the は無くても可）。

Exercise 1　次の各英文の（　　）内から適当な語（句）を選び、その記号を下の解答
　　　　　　欄に記入しなさい。

　1 Kiyoshi is（ア taller　イ tallest　ウ more tall　エ as tall) than his father.
　2 Mt. Fuji is the（ア high　イ highest　　ウ higher　　エ most high) mountain in
　　Japan.
　3 This bridge is as（ア longer　イ longest　　ウ more long　エ long) as that one.
　4 Is Japanese（ア difficult　イ more difficult　ウ most difficult　エ as difficult)
　　than Chinese?
　5 We have（ア less　イ more　ウ few　エ many) students than last year.
　6 Which sport do you like（ア more　イ better　ウ best　エ well) of all?

Answers

1＿＿＿＿＿　2＿＿＿＿＿　3＿＿＿＿＿　4＿＿＿＿＿　5＿＿＿＿＿　6＿＿＿＿＿

Exercise 2 1と2は［　　］内の語（句）を並べ替え、3〜5は日本文にあう英文を各々書いてみましょう。　　（注：文頭の文字と句読点は、要適宜対応）

1　今年の夏は去年より涼しい。　　［is, than, summer, last, this, cooler, year］

➔＿＿＿＿＿＿＿＿＿＿＿＿＿＿＿＿＿＿＿＿＿＿＿＿＿＿＿

2　これは、この美術館で一番古い絵です。

［picture, is, this museum, oldest, this, in, the］

➔＿＿＿＿＿＿＿＿＿＿＿＿＿＿＿＿＿＿＿＿＿＿＿＿＿＿＿

3　トムはそのバスに乗るためにバス停まで出来るだけ速く走った。

➔＿＿＿＿＿＿＿＿＿＿＿＿＿＿＿＿＿＿＿＿＿＿＿＿＿＿＿

4　次郎は祖父より早く起きる。実は、彼は我が家で一番早く起きる。

［ヒント：実は ☞　as a matter of fact］

➔＿＿＿＿＿＿＿＿＿＿＿＿＿＿＿＿＿＿＿＿＿＿＿＿＿＿＿

5　日本では、かつて野球はサッカーより人気があったが、今は、サッカーは日本の若者の間で野球と同じぐらい人気がでてきた。

➔＿＿＿＿＿＿＿＿＿＿＿＿＿＿＿＿＿＿＿＿＿＿＿＿＿＿＿

Coffee Break 9

co-worker	copilot	coeducation (短縮形－ co-ed)
co-founder	cosigner	coexistence	coauthor

上記クイズの答え
co-worker　同僚
copilot　副操縦士
coeducation　男女共学
co-founder　共同設立者、共同創始者
cosigner　連帯保証人（契約書等に連名でサインをする人）
coexistence　共存
coauthor　共著者（名詞）、（書籍などを）共著で著わす（動詞）

Unit 10　Hinako Shibuno - Smiling Cinderella

Ⅰ　Vocabulary Checking

A群の英単語の日本語訳をB群より選びその記号を［　　］に記入しなさい。

◆A群

1 high-fives　［　　］　　2 sweets　　　　　［　　］　　3 female ［　　］

4 gallery　　［　　］　　5 contemporaries　［　　］

◆B群

a 甘い菓子　　**b** 同世代　　**c** 女性　　**d** ハイタッチ　　**e**（ゴルフの）観衆

Ⅱ　Reading

☆ **Before Reading Passage**(Q［質問・指針］を念頭に passage［本文］を読んでみましょう)

Q1 2019年8月、何がありましたか？（誰が、何処で何をし、何故、歴史的なのか）

Q2 渋野日向子のゴルフコース上での特徴・個性とは？その理由は？

Q3 優勝し帰国後、渋野に何が起こりましたか？また彼女にとって Golden Generation（黄金世代）の存在とは？

☆ **Words & Phrases**（単語、語句のヒント）

1 enchant 〜を魅了する　　2 proceed 進む　　3 name recognition 知名　　4 rising 注目の

☆ **Passage**

It was a debut tournament abroad for twenty-year-old Japanese **female** golfer, Hinako Shibuno. In August 2019, Shibuno won the AIG Women's British Open golf tournament at Woburn in England. She was the second Japanese female golf player to win a major overseas golf tournament since Hisako Higuchi won the Women's PGA Championship in the U.S. in 1977.

During the tournament, Hinako, nicknamed '*smiling Cinderella*', [1]enchanted the gallery not only with her play on the course but with her interaction. She exchanged **high-fives** with the **gallery** between shots as she [2]proceeded to the next hole. In the winner's interview after the tournament, she replied that she occasionally and intentionally does smile and interact with the gallery to make her feel relaxed or ease her nerves. Shibuno drew laughter, replying that she was not only happy but also hungry. Not knowing the amount of the prize money[注1] £540,000, she added that she would spend some of the prize money to purchase **sweets** that she could enjoy all her life.

The fact of the matter was that Shibuno had just started her professional career only a year before this title abroad. A virtually unknown Japanese golfer who toured overseas for the first time came home as a star. A victory in the AIG British Open raised Shibuno's [3]name recognition, popularity, and media attention more than ever before. She has won sponsorship deals with several companies such as *Suntory*, *Nike* and,[注2] *Vantelin*, with which her long-time hero Tiger Woods has a contract, too.

Shibuno finished the 2019 season as the number two money-winner behind Ai Suzuki. Suzuki won seven titles that year. Both are [4]rising professional golfers in Japan. Joining them are Shibuno's other **contemporaries** in their early 20s such as Nasa Hataoka and Erika Hara who are referred to as the golden generation. Their rivalry and media attention will surely inspire Shibuno to play better while attracting the gallery with her Cinderella-like smile and interaction.

注1　£540,000（約 7200 万円）

注2　興和株式会社が発売する筋肉、関節痛等の鎮痛剤名。

Ⅲ　Listening Comprehension

Listen to the CD and choose the correct answer about the passage.

1　A　Shibuno became the second Japanese woman to win a major golf tournament abroad.

　　B　It was Shibuno's second visit to England.

　　C　Shibuno won a title for the first time in her professional golf career.

2　A　She is one of Shibuno's good rivals.

　　B　Yes, Suzuki was the biggest money winner among the women golfers in Japan.

　　C　She had won seven titles in Japan before Shibuno won the title in England.

3　A　She was surprised to hear the amount of the prize money.

　　B　She was nervous and could hardly smile.

　　C　She was hungry.

4　A　Shibuno turned professional at the age of eighteen.

　　B　Shibuno seems to enjoy interaction with the gallery while on the course.

　　C　Tiger Woods and Shibuno appeare together on the same TV commercial.

Answers　1＿＿＿＿＿＿　2＿＿＿＿＿＿　3＿＿＿＿＿＿　4＿＿＿＿＿＿

ハーフタイム

☆スマイル シンデレラ（**Smile Cinderella**）？

渋野日向子の優勝は、現地や日本の新聞などのメディアも大きく報じた。しかし、日本のメディアはプレー中も優勝インタビューも笑顔で応えた彼女をこぞって 'スマイル シンデレラ' と表現した。しかし、地元英国の The Guardian 紙や米国の主な新聞（The New York Times, The Washington Post, USA Today 他）やスポーツ専門チャンネル ESPN、Reuters（ロイター）等の表現は、いずれも 'smiling Cinderella'。'smile Cinderella' という英語表現はない。

今も日本のメディアはその表現を継続使用。英語学習の観点からは…。

IV Back to Basics（英文法の基礎）⑩ 比較 2

・ポイント 1 ☞ 「（〜の）…倍」の英語表現 ☞ times を原級や比較級の前に置いて表す。

例　This bridge is <u>three times</u> as long as that one (= bridge).

= This bridge is <u>three times</u> longer than that one.

注　「〜の 2 倍」は two times よりも twice が一般的。「2 倍の長さ」☞ twice as long as

・ポイント 2 ☞ 「（の中で）何番目」の英語表現 ☞ 序数を最上級の単語の前に置いて表す。

例　Osaka is <u>the third largest</u> city in Japan now but it used to be <u>the second largest</u> (city).

・ポイント 3 ☞ 比較級「〜より」の意味の ”to”。

a. I like English <u>better than</u> math. = I <u>prefer</u> English <u>to</u> math.［prefer A to B ☞ B より A を好む］

b. This PC is <u>better than</u> that one. = This PC is <u>superior to</u> that one.
「superior to ~ ☞ 〜より良い、優れている」。反意語句は inferior to 〜。

・ポイント 4 ☞ No + 〜人又は 物 = 「どの〜も … ない」「〜ほどの者 / 物 はいない」

a. No (other) boy speaks English as well as Kenji.

= No boy speaks English better than Kenji.

= Kenji speaks English better than any other boy.

b. No (other) mountain is as high as Mt. Fuji in Japan.

= Mt. Fuji is higher than any other mountin in Japan.

c. Nothing is as important as health.

= Nothing is more important than health.

・ポイント 5 ☞ ますます、だんだん〜 ➡ 比較級＋比較級　colder and colder / more and more interesting

・ポイント 6 ☞ はるかに、ずっと ➜ 比較級の前に much や far を置く。much better（ずっと良い）

Exercise 1 次の各英文の（　）内から適当な語（句）を選び、その記号を下の解答欄に記入しなさい。

1 I think Tom's work is（ア better　イ more　ウ better than　エ superior）to his brother's.

2 Ishikari River is the（ア third longer　イ longer than　ウ third longest　エ most long）river in Japan.

3 This road is（ア twice as wide as　イ two wider than　ウ second wider　エ twice wide as）that one.

4 He looked（ア more older　イ much older　ウ more old　エ oldest）than the last time I saw him.

5 No building（ア are as tall　イ is taller than　ウ is as tall　エ are tall）as this one in this country.

6 The singer became（ア as famous　イ more and more famous　ウ best famous　エ famous than）.

Answers

1＿＿＿＿＿　2＿＿＿＿＿　3＿＿＿＿＿　4＿＿＿＿＿　5＿＿＿＿＿　6＿＿＿＿＿

Exercise 2 1と2は［　］内の語（句）を並べ替え、3〜5は日本文にあう英文を各々書いてみましょう。　（注：文頭の文字と句読点は、要適宜対応）

1　この橋は、あの橋より長いし広い。

［wider, is, one, and, than, this bridge, longer, that］

➜ ＿＿＿＿＿＿＿＿＿＿＿＿＿＿＿＿＿＿＿＿＿＿＿＿＿＿＿＿

2　だんだん寒くなってきたが、彼は職場には車より自転車で行くのを好む。

It is［colder, driving, his office, but, to, and, biking, getting, to, colder, he, prefers］

➜ It is ＿＿＿＿＿＿＿＿＿＿＿＿＿＿＿＿＿＿＿＿＿＿＿＿＿

3　東京スカイツリーは、世界で一番高い塔です。それは東京タワーの約2倍の高さです。

［ヒント：塔 ☞ tower］

➜ ＿＿＿＿＿＿＿＿＿＿＿＿＿＿＿＿＿＿＿＿＿＿＿＿＿＿＿＿

4　花子ほど多くの本を読む女の子は彼女のクラスにはいない。

（Hanako と No で始まる二文）

➜ ＿＿＿＿＿＿＿＿＿＿＿＿＿＿＿＿＿＿＿＿＿＿＿＿＿＿＿＿

5　ロサンゼルスがアメリカで2番目に大きい都市であることは、日本では多くの人には知られていません。

➜ ＿＿＿＿＿＿＿＿＿＿＿＿＿＿＿＿＿＿＿＿＿＿＿＿＿＿＿＿

Coffee Break 10

渋野日向子のハイタッチの由来と理由は・・・

　2019 年、優勝した全英ゴルフ大会中、コース移動中にギャラリーと笑顔でハイタッチ（英語では high-five という）をして歩いた渋野。その由来はソフトボールだった。

　小学生の頃はソフトボールに熱中していた渋野。ゴルフと違いチームで戦うスポーツで、得点して本塁やベンチに戻った時、ハイタッチをしてチーム皆で喜び合ったという。

　今は個人プレーのゴルフ界の黄金世代の一人。ゴルフでもホールインワン＊やイーグル等の良いプレーができた時には、ギャラリー等と“喜びを分かち合う”ためにコース移動中に笑顔でハイタッチをするのだという。

＊2018 年６月　アース・モンダミンカップで達成。

（“独占　渋野日向子勝負の１年”　KBC テレビ /2020/3/1）

Unit 11　Carl Lewis – Sportsman of the Century

I　Vocabulary Checking

A 群の英単語（句）の日本語訳を B 群より選びその記号を［　　］に記入しなさい。

◆ A 群

　1 track and field 　［　　］　　2 invasion 　［　　］　　3 recognize 　［　　］

　4 predict 　　　　　［　　］　　5 sprint 　　［　　］

◆ B 群

　a 認める　　**b** 陸上　　**c** 侵略　　**d** 短距離（走）　　**e** 予告する

II　Reading

☆ **Before Reading Passage**(Q［質問・指針］を念頭に passage［本文］を読んでみましょう)

　Q1 伝説の陸上選手カール・ルイス─彼の生い立ち、少年の頃の彼の希望・夢は？

　Q2 カール・ルイスは、高校時代と大学時代に何を成し遂げましたか？

　Q3 ロサンゼルスオリンピックやそれ以外の五輪におけるカール・ルイスの成果とアメリカ国内外での評価は？

☆ **Words & Phrases**（単語、語句のヒント）

　1 excel 優れる　　2 western allies 西側同盟国　　3 arrogance ごう慢　　4 halt 止める　　5 run 立候補する

☆ **Passage**

Carl Lewis is considered the greatest track and field athlete of all time. Born in July 1961 in Alabama USA, his family moved to[注 1]**New Jersey** when Carl was a young boy. Although his parents wanted him to take music lessons, Carl wanted to be the best in **track and field**. His goal was to jump 25 feet in the long jump. That's about 7.6 meters! Surprisingly, he reached his goal while still in high school. Carl also [1]excelled in the 100-meter **sprint** and the 200-meter sprint.

After entering the University of Houston in Texas, Carl developed his talent. After only one year in university, he qualified for the US Olympic team in 1980. But America did not send its team to the Olympic Games in Moscow that year as a protest to the Soviet Union's **invasion** into Afganistan the previous year. U.S. [2]western allies, including Japan, joined the boycott.

Lewis, however, improved himself more in the coming years eyeing the 1984 Olympics in Los Angeles. As he **predict**ed, Lewis won four gold medals in Los Angeles. Some Americans did not like his [3]arrogance. As predicted, however, Lewis won four gold medals in the long jump, the 100-meter sprint, the 200-meter sprint, and the 400-meter relay. Still, he was not popular with Americans. Lewis was more popular in Europe and Japan where he was a hero.

Carl's medal winning streak did not [4]halt, and he would continue to raise his fame higher. Lewis won two gold medals in the 100-meter sprint and the long jump in the Seoul Olympics in 1988 and two more gold medals in the 400-meter relay and in the long jump in the 1992 Barcelona Olympics. Before retiring in 1997, he won nine gold medals and one silver medal in total in the Olympic Games and ten World Championship medals, including eight gold medals. In 1999 at the end of the 20th century, the[注2]IOC voted Carl "Sportsman of the Century". People across the world now **recognize** that Carl Lewis was the best athlete ever in his chosen sport of track and field.

Outside athletics, Carl, politically a Democrat, had tried to [5]run for pubic office in New Jersey to no avail. He had not lived there long enough to run. Having appeared in several films and TV shows including[注3]***Oprah Prime*** in 2012, Lewis is now well recognized in America.

注1 New Jersey ニュージャージー州。アメリカ北東部の州で東隣はニューヨーク州。

注2 IOC International Olympic Committee 国際オリンピック委員会

注3 Oprah Winfrey 米国で最も人気のあったテレビのトーク番組の一つ ***Oprah Winfrey Show***（1986-2011 年）の黒人女性司会者。***Oprah Prime*** は Oprah がセレブ等を招き話を聞く形式の番組（2012 年〜）。これまでに Cameron Diaz（2014 年）等が出演。

III Listening Comprehension

Listen to the CD and choose the correct answer about the passage.

1 A Yes, Lewis was born in Los Angeles in 1961.

  B in 1984

  C No, it was held in Moscow in 1980.

2 A Carl Lewis finished high school.

  B Carl Lewis entered the University of Houston.

  C Calr Lewis was chosen to be a member of the U.S. Olympic team.

3 A He won four gold medals.

  B Carl Lewis was popular in Europe and Japan.

  C None. The U.S. did not send its Olympic team there.

4 A He was good at music.

  B He has no interest in politics.

  C He was a fast runner.

Answers 1 _____ 2 _____ 3 _____ 4 _____

ハーフタイム

☆二人の著名陸上選手カール・ルイスとウサイン・ボルトのオリンピックでの獲
　得メダル総数比較

・ルイス（米国）

　10 個（金 9 ／ 100m 他）、100m 自己ベスト 9.92 秒（1988 年ソウル五輪、当時
　の世界新記録）

・ボルト（ジャマイカ）

　8 個（金 8 ／同上）、100m 9.63 秒（2012 年五輪）、自己ベスト・世界記録 9.58
　秒（2009 年ベルリン）

Ⅳ Back to Basics（英文法の基礎）⑪ 関係代名詞

関係代名詞（who, whose,whom, which, that 等）➡ 基本は、接続詞と代名詞の働きを1語で果たす。

格 先 行 詞	主　格	所 有 格	目 的 格 ＊目的格は省略可能
人	who （that）	whose	whom（that）
動物・物	which（that）	whose、（of which）	which（that）
人・物	that	——	that

★関係代名詞の決定

Step 1 独立した2文　　　　　　Yesterday I saw Mr. Smith. He teaches English at our school.

Step 2 接続詞＋代名詞の文　　　Yesterday I saw Mr. Smith and he teaches English at our school.

Step 3 関係代名詞を使った文　Yesterday I saw Mr. Smith who teaches English at our school.

・ポイント 1 ☞ 先行詞（関係詞より先に来る語）は Mr. Smith で人、そして動詞 teach の前なので主格（主語）who を使う。

Step 1 独立した2文　　　　　　This is the new car. My father bought it for me last week.

Step 2 接続詞と代名詞を含む文　This is the new car and my father bought it for me last week.

Step 3 関係代名詞を使った文　　This is the new car which my father bought for me last week.

・ポイント 2 ☞ 先行詞は the car で物、そして目的語 it の代わりなので主格ではなく目的格の which を使う。

・ポイント 3 ☞ 関係代名詞の what は「何」の意味はなく、「こと、もの」等の意味で使う。
Show me what you have in your bag. ／ I will tell you what I saw there yesterday.

・ポイント 4 ☞ 先行詞の前に every、all、the last、最上級等がある場合の関係代名詞は that!
This is the longest bridge that I have ever crossed.

Exercise 1 次の各英文の（　　　）内から適当な語(句)を選び、その記号を下の解答欄に記入しなさい。

1 I have an e-mail friend（ア whom　イ who　ウ whose　エ which）lives in New York.

2 Show me the new PC（ア what　イ whose　ウ which　エ whom）you bought yesterday.

3 Do you know the singer（ア whose　イ which　ウ what　エ that）name is Lady Gaga?

4 We liked the sandwich（ア which　イ what　ウ whom　エ of which）our mother made.

5 This is the most interesting book（ア which　イ what　ウ whose　エ that）I have ever read.

6 We cannot believe（ア which　イ what　ウ of which　エ whom）he said.

Answers

1＿＿＿＿＿　2＿＿＿＿＿　3＿＿＿＿＿　4＿＿＿＿＿　5＿＿＿＿＿　6＿＿＿＿＿

Exercise 2 1と2は［　　　］内の語（句）を並べ替え、3〜5は日本文にあう英文を各々書いてみましょう。　　（注：文頭の文字と句読点は、要適宜対応）

1　私には英語が得意な友人がいます。

[have, good at, a friend, I, is, English, who]

➔＿＿＿＿＿＿＿＿＿＿＿＿＿＿＿＿＿＿＿＿＿＿＿＿＿＿＿＿＿＿＿＿

2　昨夜、君がテレビで見た歌手がテイラー・スイフトです。

［saw, was, whom, on TV, the singer, Taylor Swift, you, last night］

➔＿＿＿＿＿＿＿＿＿＿＿＿＿＿＿＿＿＿＿＿＿＿＿＿＿＿＿＿＿＿＿＿

3　その警官はサングラスをかけたその不審者にバッグの中（に持っている物）を見せるように言った。

➔＿＿＿＿＿＿＿＿＿＿＿＿＿＿＿＿＿＿＿＿＿＿＿＿＿＿＿＿＿＿＿＿

4　僕は前の晩に勝ったチームの名前を思い出せなかった。

➔＿＿＿＿＿＿＿＿＿＿＿＿＿＿＿＿＿＿＿＿＿＿＿＿＿＿＿＿＿＿＿＿

5　その戦争で両親と兄弟を亡くしたその幼い男の子は、誰が世話をするのですか。

［ヒント：亡くした ☞ 殺害された］

➔＿＿＿＿＿＿＿＿＿＿＿＿＿＿＿＿＿＿＿＿＿＿＿＿＿＿＿＿＿＿＿＿

Coffee Break 11

✪次の1〜6の英語にあたる日本語は下記 a 〜 f のどれでしょう。

（答はこのページ下）

1 sit up   2 push up   3 high jump

4 shot put   5 pole vault   6 triple jump

a 砲丸投げ　b 三段跳び　c 腹筋運動　d 棒高跳び　e 腕立て伏せ　f 高飛び

上記の答

1 c   2 e   3 f   4 a   5 d   6 b

photo by Darren Wilkinson

Unit 12　Sani Brown Loves Sunny Florida

I　Vocabulary Checking

A群の英単語の日本語訳をB群より選びその記号を〔　　〕に記入しなさい。

◆A群

1 produce 〔　　〕　　2 anxiety 〔　　〕　　3 flexibility 〔　　〕

4 commit 〔　　〕　　5 establish 〔　　〕

◆B群

a 柔軟性　　**b** ～を築く　　**c** 心配、不安　　**d** 輩出する　　**e** 真剣に取り組む

II　Reading

☆ **Before Reading Passage**(Q［質問・指針］を念頭に passage［本文］を読んでみましょう)

Q1 Sani Brown とは誰ですか？高校時代、何故、彼は世界的にも注目されたのですか？

Q2 Sani Brown の高校卒業後の進路希望と結果は？

Q3 Sani Brown にとってフロリダ大学はどんな大学ですか。

☆ **Words & Phrases**（単語、語句のヒント）

1 sprint 短距離走　2 enroll 在籍する　3 outweigh ～に勝る　4 scores of 数十人の　5 stardom スターの地位

☆ **Passage**

Abdul Hakim Sani Brown is one of Japan's top athletes specializing in the men's 100m and 200m [1]sprints. Another sprinter Yoshihide Kiryu, the first Japanese to break the 10 second barrier in the 100m race, is one of his rivals as well as a teammate in the 400m relay. Although Kiryu clocked 9.98 seconds in September 2017, Sani Brown would break the national record in less than two years.

Sani Brown was born in Kitakyushu in March 1999 to a[注1]Ghanaian father and a Japanese mother, who was once a sprinter. He went to Jōsai High School in Tokyo where he **established** fame as a star sprinter. In 2015 at the age of 16, he received the Rising Star Award from the[注2]IAAF. He won two gold medals in the 100m and 200m races at the 2015 IAAF World Youth Championships held in Colombia. After high school, Sani Brown longed to be [2]enrolled at a university that could provide him with better academic support and a high-level of training in track. He found it in America. His ambition to improve himself [3]outweighed his **anxiety** about the language barrier and cultural differences abroad. In the fall of 2017, he entered the University of

Florida in Gainsville.

His decision was right. The University of Florida has **produced** many top U.S. athletes, including ⁴scores of Olympic medalists. Among its alumni are Bernard Williams, the gold medalist in the 200m sprint at the 2004 Athens Olympics and Tony McQuay, the gold medalist in the 400m relay at the 2016 Rio de Janeiro Olympics. Sani Brown liked the outstanding coaches and the high-level track and field training program at the university, which he could hardly have found in Japan. He **commited** himself to various training programs there to improve his strength and **flexibility**. He gained weight in his hips and thighs, an important factor for sprinters.

Sani Brown's efforts paid off soon. In June 2019, he set a new Japanese record of 9.97 seconds in the 100m race in the注³NCAA championships in Austin, Texas. His ⁵stardom as a sprinter has now risen on to the world stage. Sani Brown will stay commited to improving his skill, speed, and strength.

注1　Ghanaian ガーナ人　ガーナ共和国（Republic of Ghana）アフリカ西部の国

注2　IAAF（International Association of Athletics Federations, 国際陸上競技連盟）。2019 年秋、改称し World Athletics（WA）に。日本では通称、世界陸連。

注3　NCAA（National Collegiate Athletic Association）全米大学体育協会。

Ⅲ　Listening Comprehension

Listen to the CD and choose the correct answer about the passage.

1　A　He was born in Kitakyushu but was mostly brought up in Tokyo.

　　B　He has visited Colombia.

　　C　Sani Brown became famous after he finished high school.

2　A　in 2017 in Gainsville, Florida

　　B　No, it was in 2015 in Colombia.

　　C　It was in Austin, Texas.

3　A　He worked hard in the program, which seemed to have led him to a new national record.

　　B　Yes, he met some coaches who had trained some Olympic medalists.

　　C　He liked the training program at the University of Texas at Austin, too.

4　A　Kiryu is the first Japanese sprinter to run the 100m sprint in less than ten seconds.

　　B　Sani Brown's weight hardly changed after entering the University of Florida.

　　C　Cultural differences were not a big problem for Sani Brown in deciding to train abroad.

Answers　1＿＿＿＿＿＿　2＿＿＿＿＿＿　3＿＿＿＿＿＿　4＿＿＿＿＿＿

ハーフタイム

IV　Back to Basics（英文法の基礎）⑫　形容詞と副詞

- ポイント 1 形容詞は名詞（人や動物、又は物等の名前等）の形、容姿、性質、状態等を述べる語。

　　　形容詞は、飾る（修飾する）名詞の前や後にくる場合、単独で動詞の後にくる場合などがある。

　・名詞の前にくる例　　Mary is a <u>pretty</u> girl. / Tom likes the <u>new</u> car.

　　　　　　　　　　　　We like the <u>new</u> <u>young</u> doctor.

　・名詞の後にくる例　　Give me something <u>cold</u> to drink.

　・動詞の後にくる例　　You look <u>happy</u>. / Nancy is <u>kind</u> and <u>beautiful</u>.

　・数量を表わす例　　　<u>How many</u> books are there in the room?　There are <u>some</u> books.

- ポイント 2 副詞は動詞や形容詞、更に別の副詞を修飾する。つづりは '形容詞＋ly' が多い。

　・Tom spoke <u>slowly</u>. / Mary left the room <u>quietly</u>. / He finished the work <u>easily</u>.

　・He drove the car <u>very</u> <u>carefully</u>. （very は副詞 carefully を、carefully は動詞 drove を修飾）

　・We <u>often</u> play tennis there. 　/ 　My father <u>never</u> drinks alcohol.

　　＊ often, always, sometimes 等の頻度を表わす語は助動詞や be 動詞の後、一般動詞の前におく。

- ポイント 3 同じ単語で形容詞と副詞のある語、意味も品詞も違う語がある。

　・Tom is a <u>fast</u> runner. ［fast は名詞 runner を飾る形容詞］/ Tom can run <u>fast</u>. ［fast は動詞 run を飾る副詞］

　・This test is <u>hard</u>. ［難しい☞形容詞］/The ground is <u>hard</u>. ［堅い☞形容詞］/ Tom works <u>hard</u>. ［懸命に☞副詞］

　　＊ I can <u>hardly</u> speak English. ［hardly は hard とは別単語で、「ほとんどない（副詞）」の意

Exercise 1 次の各英文の（　　）内から適当な語（句）を選び、その記号を下の解答欄に記入しなさい。

1 The (ア boy tall　イ tall boy　ウ tall boys　エ tall a boy) is my brother Kenji.

2 My grandma is 70 years old but looks (ア a young　イ young very　ウ young エ young lady).

3 Give me (ア hot something　イ hot anything　ウ something hot　エ more hot) to drink..

4 I could run (ア more fast　イ fastly　ウ early　エ fast) when I was young.

5 There are (ア much　イ more than　ウ a little　エ many) books in the library.

6 My father (ア often plays　イ is often player　ウ plays often　エ can often plays) golf there.

Answers

1＿＿＿＿＿　2＿＿＿＿＿　3＿＿＿＿＿　4＿＿＿＿＿　5＿＿＿＿＿　6＿＿＿＿＿

Exercise 2 1と2は［　　］内の語（句）を並べ替え、3〜5は日本文にあう英文を各々書いてみましょう。　　　（注：文頭の文字と句読点は、要適宜対応）

1　彼女は、いつもその新しいスーパーで買い物をします。

　　　　　　[always, her, at, she, the new,　does, supermarket, shopping]

→＿＿＿＿＿＿＿＿＿＿＿＿＿＿＿＿＿＿＿＿＿＿＿＿＿＿＿＿＿＿＿＿＿＿＿

2　私の姉は数年ニューヨークで過ごしたので英語を上手に話す。

　　　　[speaks, in New York, years, well, spent, my sister, some, English, and]

→＿＿＿＿＿＿＿＿＿＿＿＿＿＿＿＿＿＿＿＿＿＿＿＿＿＿＿＿＿＿＿＿＿＿＿

3　彼は一生懸命勉強したのでやっと難関の司法試験に合格できた。

　　　　　　　　　　　　　　　　　　　[ヒント：司法試験 ☞ bar exam]

→＿＿＿＿＿＿＿＿＿＿＿＿＿＿＿＿＿＿＿＿＿＿＿＿＿＿＿＿＿＿＿＿＿＿＿

4　その講師はとても速く話したので、我々は彼の話をほとんど理解できなかった。

　　　　　　　　　　　　　　　　　　　　[ヒント：講師☞ lecturer]

→＿＿＿＿＿＿＿＿＿＿＿＿＿＿＿＿＿＿＿＿＿＿＿＿＿＿＿＿＿＿＿＿＿＿＿

5　ファーストフードばかり食べて（食べ続けて）運動もほとんどしないと太るよ。

→＿＿＿＿＿＿＿＿＿＿＿＿＿＿＿＿＿＿＿＿＿＿＿＿＿＿＿＿＿＿＿＿＿＿＿

Coffee Break 12

－ 陸上競技のスタートの合図 －

・日本語　　位置について！　　用意！　　　ドン！
　　　　　　　　　↓　　　　　　　↓　　　　　↓
・英　語　　On your mark !　　Get set !　　Go !

Unit 13　Yuzuru Hanyu – Prince on Ice

photo by David W. Carmichael - davecskatingphoto.com.

I　Vocabulary Checking

A群の英単語の日本語訳をB群より選びその記号を〔　　〕に記入しなさい。

◆A群

1 award　　〔　　〕　　2 competition　　〔　　〕　　3 quadruple　　〔　　〕

4 consider　〔　　〕　　5 accomplishments〔　　〕

◆B群

a 競技、大会　　**b** 4回の　　**c** ～と見なす　　**d** 賞（を授ける）　　**e** 功績、偉業

II　Reading

☆ **Before Reading Passage**(Q［質問・指針］を念頭に passage［本文］を読んでみましょう)

Q1 フィギュアスケーター羽生結弦選手の成績・記録をまとめてみましょう。

Q2 羽生結弦選手は、いつ何故、国民栄誉賞を授与されたのでしょう。

☆ **Words & Phrases**（単語、語句のヒント）

1 immensely 非常に　　2 throne 王位　　3 limelight 脚光　　4 back-to-back 連続して　　5 awe 崇拝、畏敬

☆ **Passage**

Figure skating **competition** is an ¹immensely popular spectator sport in Japan. People go nuts over the top figure skaters, especially if they are from Japan. The figure skater that now sits atop the ²throne of global popularity is Yuzuru Hanyu, the world number one ranked male figure skater. Hanyu is **considered** one of the best figure skaters of all time.

Hanyu was born in December 1994 in Sendai. He started skating at a young age, about four. From his late teens and to the present, Hanyu has been in the ³limelight as one of the most popular male figure skaters worldwide as he has kept winning numerous **award**s in men's singles competitions. These include two Olympic gold medals, two World Championships, four Grand Prix Final championships, and four Japanese national championships. Also, Hanyu is the only male skater to have won a Super Slam. This means he has won all major competitions in both his junior and senior careers. He has broken world records 19 times, which is nothing but incredible! There was a competition in 2016 where Hanyu nailed a **quadruple** loop. This was the first time any skater had successfully done this in competition.

Notable of all, however, Hanyu became the first Asian (and Japanese) figure skater competing in men's singles to win a gold medal in the Winter Olympics. This was in 2014 in Sochi, Russia. He also won the gold in the 2018 Winter Olympics in Pyeong Chang, South Korea. He is the first male singles competitor to do so since Dick Button won [4]back-to-back gold medals in 1948 and 1952. Surprisingly enough, Hanyu was off the ice rink for a couple of months after an injury in November 2017. It was not surprising after the Olympics that he was awarded the[注] People's Honor Award in July 2018 for his great **accomplishments**, giving the Japanese people hope and courage. He was the youngest ever to receive the award.

Yuzuru loves earphones. In fact, it seems to be an obsession of his. He listens to music before competition. This gets him focused and pumped up to compete well.

Yuzuru continues to strike [5]awe into spectators from around the world. He has made his mark in figure skating and is a true sports hero and a living legend.

注　the People's Honor Award 国民栄誉賞　1977 年創設された内閣総理大臣表彰のひとつ。広く国民に敬愛され、社会に明るい希望を与えることに顕著な業績があった者に与えられる。

III　Listening Comprehension

CD
27

Listen to the CD and choose the correct answer about the passage.

1　A　in his late teens

　　B　probably in 1998

　　C　He was born in Sendai in 1994.

2　A　No, it was in 2014 that Hanyu won the gold medal in Sochi, Russia.

　　B　Hanyu successfully jumped a quadruple, the first figure skater ever to do so.

　　C　Hanyu stayed away from the ice rink for about two months due to an injury.

3　A　Because he won the gold medals in the Olympics in 2014 and 2018.

　　B　Because he won a Super Slam, the first figure skater to do so.

　　C　Yes, he won the gold medal in the 2018 Winter Olympics in Pyeong Chang, South Korea.

4　A　Yuzuru was a rising star on the world stage before he turned twenty.

　　B　No male figure skater has won two gold medals in the winter Olympics except Hanyu.

　　C　Yuzuru seems to enjoy music through earphones before competition.

Answers　1 ＿＿＿＿＿　2 ＿＿＿＿＿　3 ＿＿＿＿＿　4 ＿＿＿＿＿

ハーフタイム

☆あっぱれ！　　小平奈緒は **Role Model!**

　日本女子スピードスケートの第一人者の小平奈緒。2018 年、平昌オリンピックでは女子スピードスケート 500 m で五輪新記録で金メダルに輝いた。

　滑り終わった直後、観客の拍手に応えるも直ぐに指を唇に当て「お静かに」のしぐさ。後に続く選手が競技に集中できるように、との彼女の気遣いだった。フェアプレーに徹したアスリートのお手本（role model）。この気遣いにも金メダル！

Ⅳ　Back to Basics（英文法の基礎）⑬　分詞と動名詞

☆分　詞　　現在分詞（動詞＋ing）と過去分詞（動詞＋ed の規則変化と不規則変化の 2 通り）がある。

☆動名詞　　動詞の語尾に 'ing' がつき、その動詞が名詞化した語をいう。

・ポイント 1 現在分詞 ⟶ 'be 動詞＋動詞 ing' の形で進行形に使う以外に、主に名詞の前後に置き「～している」「～しながら」等と訳す。

　　　例　the sleeping cat ／ some boys playing soccer over there

　　　　　the boy sitting in the chair

　　　　　I saw Tom crossing the street.（横断中の）

　　　　　She went out of the room crying.（泣きながら）

・ポイント 2 過去分詞 ⟶ 'be 動詞＋過去分詞'（受動態）や 'have（has）＋過去分詞'（完了形）の形で使う以外に、主に名詞の前後に置き「～された、される」等と訳す。

　　　例　the broken chair ／ the watch made in Japan

　　　　　the language spoken in Canada

　　　　　I found my car stolen last week.　／ I heard my name called.

・ポイント 3 動名詞 ⟶ 形は現在分詞と同じだが、意味は普通「～すること」等と訳す。

　　　例　The baby stopped crying. ／ Mary is good at cooking.

　　　　　My hobby is listening to jazz.

Exercise 1 次の各英文の（　　）内から適当な語（句）を選び、その記号を下の解答
欄に記入しなさい。

1 （ア Collecting　イ Collect　ウ To be collected　エ To collecting) coins is interesting.

2 I saw some boys（ア to play　イ playing　ウ be playing　エ played) soccer in the park.

3 It started（ア rain　イ rained　ウ to raining　エ raining) in the evening.

4 Here are the dishes（ア broke　イ broken　ウ breaking　エ be broken) by Mary.

5 The lady（ア wearing　イ worn　ウ to wear　エ being worn) the red hat is my aunt.

6 The old man is very proud of（ア is　イ be　ウ been　エ being) very rich.

Answers

1_____　2_____　3_____　4_____　5_____　6_____

Exercise 2　1と2は［　　］内の語（句）を並べ替え、3〜5は日本文にあう英文を
各々書いてみましょう。　　　　　　（注：文頭の文字と句読点は、要適宜対応）

1　先月、父が僕に中古車（＝使われた車）を買ってくれた。

[month, me, a, my father, car, bought, last, used]

→ _____

2　うちの娘は、祖母と買い物に行くのがとても好きです。

[with, of, is, her grandma, going, our daughter, very, shopping, fond]

→ _____

3　同僚からの電話の後、彼は一言も言わずに部屋を去っていった。

[ヒント：同僚 ☞ colleague]

→ _____

4　その待合室はとても騒がしくて、私は自分の名前が呼ばれたのがほとんど聞こえな
かった。　　　　　　　　　　　　[ヒント：待合室　☞ waiting room]

→ _____

5　あの角を右に曲がると、約500年前に建てられたお寺が見えます。

→ _____

Coffee Break 13

冬季オリンピック

　1924 年 フランスのシャモニーでの開催が最初。1994 年、リレハンメル（ノルウェー）大会から夏季オリンピックの中間の年に開催されることになった。2020 年現在、冬季オリンピックの南半球での開催はない。

　なお、1896 年、アテネ（ギリシャ）で始まり 4 年毎に開催される夏季オリンピックの開催年は閏（うるう）年とアメリカ大統領選挙と同じ年に開催されるので覚えやすい。

Unit 14　King Kazu - J. League Pioneer

I　Vocabulary Checking

A群の英単語の日本語訳をB群より選びその記号を［　　］に記入しなさい。

◆A群

1 overseas ［　　］　　2 award ［　　］　　3 enrich ［　　］

4 childhood ［　　］　　5 outstanding ［　　］

◆B群

a ～を積み上げる、豊富にする　　**b** 幼少時　　**c** 輝かしい　　**d** 賞　　**e** 海外で

II　Reading

☆ **Before Reading Passage**（Q［質問・指針］を念頭に passage［本文］を読んでみましょう）

Q1 サッカーのJリーガー カズ（三浦知良）のJリーグデビューまでの経歴をまとめてみましょう。

Q2 Jリーガー カズにとって、1993年はどういう年でしたか？

Q3 Jリーガー カズの1994年以降の実績、存在理由についてまとめてみましょう。

☆ **Words & Phrases**（単語、語句のヒント）

1 deserves ～に値する　2 popularize ～を広める　3 remain ～し続ける　4 active 現役の　5 admit ～と認める

☆ **Passage**

Kazuyoshi Miura is a legendary soccer player. He ¹deserves credit for ²popularizing professional soccer in Japan. Born in Shizuoka City in 1967, Miura, sometimes called Kazu or King Kazu, started playing soccer in his **childhood**. In December 1982, he dropped out of high school after attending less than a year and went to Brazil to be a professional player. In 1986, he signed his first professional contract with Santos. Kazu later returned in 1990 hoping to play in Japan.

In 1993, Miura made a dramatic debut as captain of Verdi Kawasaki, with the start of the Japan Professional Football League, known as J. League. In July, he received the MVP **award** in the All-Star game. To make himself even happier, Kazu married Risako Shitara, an actress, the next month. The 1993 season ended with the championship for Verdi, for which Kazu received the first J. League MVP award. He also received the Japan Professional Sports Grand Prize that year. His successful career continued for several years, leading Verdi to the Emperor's Cup in January 1997. He scored 100 goals in 2000, a first in the J. League. Also Kazu **enrich**ed his career by playing **overseas**. He played as the first Japanese soccer player to play in Italy in 1994, in Croatia in 1998, and in Australia in 2005.

Having played for Yokohama FC since 2005, Kazu continues to ³remain in the spotlight. In 2007, he played in the J-League All Star Soccer for the J-East impressing many fans. Ten years later in 2017, Miura added another record to his career in a J-League 2 match against Thespa Kusatsu Gunma. Kazu scored the only goal in the game, becoming the oldest professional goalscorer by breaking the record held since 1965 by an English footballer Sir Stanley Mattews. Kazu showed well his high mentality as well as high-level physical talent at the age of fifty.

As of 2020, Kazu, the oldest ⁴active J. League player, ⁵admits that he has little room to physically improve. Kazu has left **outstanding** records and has attracted and impressed many fans. His dedication to J-League for almost three decades has now become an important part of his legacy. And the legacy will always be remembered even after King Kazu leaves the football pitch for good.

注　J. League 1 に限定すると元ブラジル代表のジーコの 41 歳 3 ケ月 12 日がある。

Ⅲ　Listening Comprehension

Listen to the CD and choose the correct answer about the passage.

1　A　He played in Santos, Brazil.
　　B　He left high school to live in Italy as the first Japanese professional soccer player there.
　　C　He went to Brazil.

2　A　He signed the contract in 1986.
　　B　Kazu married Risako Shitara in August, 1993.
　　C　Yes, Kazu married Risako Shitara, an actress.

3　A　He returned in 1990 hoping to play in Japan.
　　B　to play in the Emperor's Cup in 1997
　　C　In 1993, Kazu returned to sing with *Verdi* Kawasaki.

4　A　At the age of fifty, Kazu set a new record.
　　B　Kazu made 100 goals in the year 2000 alone.
　　C　Kazu has played in the J-League for almost thirty years.

Answers　1 _____　2 _____　3 _____　4 _____

ハーフタイム

☆よく耳にする **MVP** と **VIP** の違いは？

MVP ・・・most valuable player の略で「最も価値のある / 活躍した選手」

VIP ・・・very important person の略で「非常に重要な人。首相や大統領等」

IV Back to Basics（英文法の基礎）⑭ 前置詞

☆前置詞は、その後に来る名詞や名詞相当語（句）と一緒になり2語以上で、形容詞、副詞の働きをする。

主な前置詞 ☞ at, along, by, down, during, for, from, in, into, of, off, on, over, to, under, up, with 等。

・ポイント **1** 時に関する前置詞

a. at ☞ 瞬間的時間 　　　例 Come here at nine. / The train left at 6:30.

b. in ☞ 月、年、一定期間 　例 in May, in 2013、in the morning / afternoon / evening （*at night）

c. on ☞ 曜日等 　　　　　例 on Sunday, on Friday morning, on the morning of May 3rd

d. for ☞ 具体的期間 　　　例 for two days, for one and half hours, for weeks（数週間）, for years

e. during ☞ 期間中（ずっと）例 during (the) winter, during the meal, during (the) summer vacation

注 Wait here until noon.［until：〜まで］と Come here by noon.［by：〜までに］。

・ポイント **2** 場所に関する前置詞

a. in（中に☞状態）/ into（中へ☞動作）

例 in the room, in the city / into the room （⇔ out of the room）

b. to（〜 へ ☞ 方向）、in（広い場所に ［到着］）at（狭い場所に ［到着］）、for（目的地に向け）

例 go to Paris、arrive in Paris / at the station、leave for Tokyo

c. on （接して上）/ over（離れて真上）

例 on the table 　/ over the river （⇔ under the bridge）

d. up（上へ）/ down（下へ）

例 go up / down the stairs 階段を上ぼる / 降りる

e. between two trees（2本の木の間）/ among men（3人以上の男性の間）

74

Exercise 1

1 I was born (ア in　イ on　ウ at　エ for) October 19, 1998.

2 We played soccer (ア for　イ during　ウ on　エ from) three hours yesterday.

3 Will you finish the work (ア until　イ at　ウ in　エ by) tomorrow?

4 The lady has lived in the city (ア for　イ from　ウ since　エ at) many years.

5 We had two English lessons (ア on　イ in　ウ at　エ of) the morning.

6 My father goes to work (ア at　イ in　ウ by　エ on) subway.

Answers

1＿＿＿＿＿＿　2＿＿＿＿＿＿　3＿＿＿＿＿＿　4＿＿＿＿＿＿　5＿＿＿＿＿＿　6＿＿＿＿＿＿

Exercise 2　1と2は［　　］内の語（句）を並べ替え、3～5は日本文にあう英文を
　　　　　　　各々書いてみましょう。　　　　（注：文頭の文字と句読点は、要適宜対応）

1　ある老婆が公園のベンチに座っていた。

[an, the park, was, the bench, old lady, on, sitting, in]

→＿＿＿＿＿＿＿＿＿＿＿＿＿＿＿＿＿＿＿＿＿＿＿＿＿＿＿＿＿＿＿＿＿＿＿

2　私の姉はリビングルームに入って来て、彼女のバッグをテーブルの上に置きました。

[her bag, into, the table, put, came, on, my sister, and, the living room]

→＿＿＿＿＿＿＿＿＿＿＿＿＿＿＿＿＿＿＿＿＿＿＿＿＿＿＿＿＿＿＿＿＿＿＿

3　そのセミナーは午後1時に始まり3時から10分の休憩があった。

→＿＿＿＿＿＿＿＿＿＿＿＿＿＿＿＿＿＿＿＿＿＿＿＿＿＿＿＿＿＿＿＿＿＿＿

4　何らかの理由で電車が時間通りに出なかったので、僕は今朝、その会議に遅れてし
　　まった。

→＿＿＿＿＿＿＿＿＿＿＿＿＿＿＿＿＿＿＿＿＿＿＿＿＿＿＿＿＿＿＿＿＿＿＿

5　その川には3つの橋が架かっています。そのうちの一つは先月の台風で被害をうけ
　　今、工事中です。

［ヒント：～に架かる ☞ over、被害 ☞ damage、（被害を）うける ☞ cause、工事
中 ☞ under construction ］

→＿＿＿＿＿＿＿＿＿＿＿＿＿＿＿＿＿＿＿＿＿＿＿＿＿＿＿＿＿＿＿＿＿＿＿

Coffee Break 14

フットボールはサッカー？

　日米ではサッカーというのが一般的。しかし、イギリス等ではフットボールと言うのが一般的。アメリカでフットボールと言うと American football のことで誤解をまねきかねないので要注意である。

　そういえば、国際サッカー連盟は FIFA と言われる。仏語の Federation International de Football Association の略で、英語でも The International Federation of Association Football。いずれも soccer という語ではなく football が使用されている。ということは、soccer と言う方がマイナー（minor）で、football がメジャー（major）？（@ _ @ ;）

Unit 15　Gender Inequality in Sports

I　Vocabulary Checking

A群の英単語の日本語訳をB群より選びその記号を［　　］に記入しなさい。

◆A群

1 conduct　　［　　］　　　2 currently　［　　］　　　3 progress　　　［　　　］

4 backwards［　　］　　　5 displeased［　　］

◆B群

a 行い　　**b** 進展、進歩　　**c** 不満な、不機嫌な　　**d** 前後逆　　**e** 現在は

II　Reading

CD
30

☆ **Before Reading Passage**(Q［質問・指針］を念頭に passage［本文］を読んでみましょう)

Q1 スポーツは、何故、世界中の人々を魅了し、また多くの人達に親しまれているのでしょうか？

Q2 Alizé Cornet とは誰ですか？ 2018 年、何故、彼女は話題になったのでしょうか？

Q3 スポーツの世界での男女平等の進捗状況—進んだ例と未達の例を挙げてみましょう。

☆ **Words & Phrases**（単語、語句のヒント）

1 resolve 解決する　　2 inadvertently うっかり　　3 affect 影響する　　4 explicit 明確な　　5 regrettable 残念な

☆ **Passage**

　Sports can be enjoyed by many people around the world. Sport does not consider age, gender, nationality, ethnicity, or religion. It does not matter whether you are rich or poor, from the city or from the countryside. Some participants may even become professional. Regardless of whether a person is professional or amateur, players compete with each other under the same rules and conditions. Sports do have some issues to be ¹resolved.

　Gender inequality in sports has sometimes drawn some attention. It happened in the U.S. Open tennis tournament in New York in 2018. Alizé Cornet, a female French tennis player, was given a code violation for changing her top on court which she had ²inadvertently worn **backwards**. The umpire regarded her **conduct** as unsportsmanlike behavior. **Displeased** with the decision, Cornet expressed her anger by saying, "Violation for what? Really?" The decision, however, was not changed and the match continued without ³affecting the score. While men were free to change their shirts on court, women were not, an ⁴explicit gender divide. The U.S.

Tennis Association in charge of the U.S. Open later stated that the decision was [5]regrettable, a simple error by the umpire. No further penalty was given to Cornet. This episode once again spotlighted a double standard considering gender in sports.

On the other hand, gender equality has made **progress** in some areas. In professional sports, the amount of the prize money once differed greatly between men and women. In the grand slam tournaments in tennis, for example, men's and women's singles champions **currently** receive equal prize money. But it was not until 1973 at the U.S. Open that the prize money first became equal between men and women. And it took almost three decades or more for other grand slam tournaments to follow suit, 2001 for the Australian Open, 2006 for the French Open, and Wimbledon in 2007. In professional golf, prize money differences still exist. Differing in the course, the man's champion of the British Open received over £1.5 million in 2019 while the woman's champion of the AIG British Open £540,000. Gender equality in sports has progressed but still has a long way to go.

III Listening Comprehension

Listen to the CD and choose the correct answer about the passage.

1   A   The U.S. Tennis Association is responsible for the U.S. Open.
    B   She wore her top the wrong way by mistake and changed it on court.
    C   Once a tennis player, Cornet now is an umpire for the U.S. Open.

2   A   Because she thought changing her top on court was not wrong.
    B   Because she could not win the title as expected.
    C   Because the umpire changed his decision only after the game.

3   A   Some rules for professional tennis players were changed about their shirts.
    B   The U.S Tennis Association said that the umpire made an error.
    C   The champion's prize money at the French Open became equal between men and women.

4   A   No double standards in sports seem to exist in gender any more.
    B   The umpire did not change his decision even after Cornet showed her displeasure.
    C   The issue of gender equality in sports came to be discussed after 1973.

Answers 1 _____ 2 _____ 3 _____ 4 _____

ハーフタイム

☆優勝賞金の男女同額は平等？不平等？

　テニスのグランドスラムは４大会ともシングル優勝賞金は男女とも同額。だが、一部選手の間では不満、異論があるようだ。

◆ジル・シモン（仏男）選手らの言い分

　「男子は（最大）５セット戦うが女子は３セットまで。」「男子テニスのレベルが女子より先行している。」

◆マリア・シャラポア（露女。2019年引退）選手らの反論

　「私の試合を（上記男子の試合）より多くの人が観ており大会に貢献している。」この意見にセリーナ・ウィリアムズ（米）も賛同。

（日経　8/31/2015）

Ⅳ　Back to Basics（英文法の基礎）⑮　it の用法　と　否定

【1】it の用法 ・・・ "それ" という意味・働き（代名詞）以外の用法について。

・ポイント 1 ☞　話題が「天気・気候」「時間」「距離」等の文の主語として使う。

　・天気　It was rainy yesterday but it is fine today.　/　It is snowing and it is very cold.

　・時間　What time is it now?　It is five thirty.　/　It is getting late. Let's go home.

　・距離　How far is it from here to the bus stop?　It is only two blocks from here.

・ポイント 2 ☞ 仮の主語や目的語　➡ 主語や目的語が長い場合にその代わりに使う。

　・It is not easy for me to finish the work in a day.（to 以下が本来の主語）

　・It is true that time is money.（time 以下の部分が本来の主語）

　・We think it better to say nothing about the accident.（to 以下が think の本来の目的語）

【2】否 定

・little と few　　意味 ☞「ほとんど～ない」。共に、very little, very few と表現する場合もある。

　・ポイント 1 few は、数えることが可能（可算）な語に、little は、数えられない語（不可算）につく。

　　　例　I saw few students there.　/　We had little snow this winter.

・hardly, seldom, rarely　　意味☞「ほとんど～ない」「めったに～しない」

　・ポイント 2 hardly は程度等が「ほとんど～ない」、seldom、rarely は頻度が「めったに～ない」。

　　　例 We can hardly understand his story.

　　　　My father seldom/ rarely watches TV.

- 全部否定と部分否定、否定文の「も」
  - ポイント 3 100%を意味する語（all, both, always, every 等）＋not ☞ 部分否定。

  例 I don't know all of them. （彼らのうち何人かを知らない－部分否定）

  ⇔ I know none of them. （彼ら全員を知らない－全部否定）

  I don't know both of his parents.

  （両親の一方のみを知っている－部分否定）

  ⇔ I know neither of his parents.

  （両親の両方とも知らない－全部否定）

  ＝ I don't know either of his parents.

  I don't always get up at seven.

  （いつも 7 時起床ではない－部分否定）

  ⇔ I never get up at seven. （7時に起きることはない－全部否定）

  Not everyone knows him.

  （皆が彼を知っているわけではない－部分否定）

  ⇔ No one（又は Nobody）knows him.

  （誰も彼を知らない－全部否定）

  - ポイント 4 否定文の「～も」は too ではなく either。

  例 You don't like rock music. I don't like rock music, <u>either</u>.

Exercise 1

1 We found（ア that イ it ウ us エ too）difficult to finish the work by tomorrow.

2 None of his work（ア has イ have ウ being エ is）been done yet.

3 My sister doesn't like dogs. I don' t like them,（ア too イ neither ウ also エ either）.

4 We have（ア little イ few ウ many エ hardly）tea left in the pot.

5 Tom（ア little イ seldom ウ hardly エ none）eats breakfast.

Answers

1＿＿＿＿＿＿ 2＿＿＿＿＿＿ 3＿＿＿＿＿＿ 4＿＿＿＿＿＿ 5＿＿＿＿＿＿

Exercise 2 1と2は［　　］内の語（句）を並べ替え、3〜5は日本文にあう英文を各々書いてみましょう。　　　　（注：文頭の文字と句読点は、要適宜対応）

1　誰もその話が本当かどうか知らない。

[one, is, or, the story, if, knows, no, not, true]

→ _____

2　僕の友人は誰も車を持っていない。　　　　[of, has, my, a car, none, friends]

→ _____

3　この部屋はとても暑いです。窓を開けてもいいですか。

→ _____

4　暗くなってきたね。ここから今夜、私達が滞在するホテルまであとどれくらい時間かかるの。

→ _____

5　その事故については、今は、我々は何も言わないでおくのが良いと僕は思う。

→ _____

Coffee Break 15

なでしこジャパン（女子サッカーチーム）の帰国便がビジネスクラスに！

　2012年ロンドン・オリンピックで銀メダルを獲得した女子サッカーチームの帰国便が往路便のエコノミークラスからビジネスクラスに格上げされた。銀メダル獲得へのご褒美だった。男子サッカーの選手は、往路便はビジネスクラス。男女同等に一歩前進？

　サッカーのワールドカップでは女子が男子より先に優勝している（2011年7月）

テキストの音声は、弊社 HP
http://www.eihosha.co.jp/の
「テキスト音声ダウンロード」
のバナーからダウンロードでき
ます。

Attention All Sports Fans!
「アスリート、スポーツの世界と英語の基礎固め」

2021年1月15日　初　版

著　者© M a r k　T h o m p s o n
谷　岡　敏　博

発 行 者　佐　々　木　　元

発 行 所　株式会社　英　　宝　　社

〒 101-0032 東京都千代田区岩本町 2-7-7
☎ [03] (5833) 5870　Fax [03] (5833) 5872

ISBN 978-4-269-42062-5 C1082
製版・印刷・製本：モリモト印刷株式会社
表紙デザイン：伊谷企画